Fund Raising and Grant Aid for Voluntary Organisations

A Guide to the Literature

Compiled by Susan Bates

BEDFORD SQUARE PRESS | NCVO

Published by
BEDFORD SQUARE PRESS of the
National Council for Voluntary Organisations
26 Bedford Square, London WC1B 3HU

© NCVO 1981, 1986

ISBN 0 7199 1154 0

First published 1981
Reprinted 1982
Reprinted 1984
Second edition 1986

Typeset by D P Media Limited, Hitchin, Hertfordshire

Printed and bound in England by Billing & Sons Limited, Worcester

Contents

Acknowledgements

I would like to thank the Charities Aid Foundation and the John S. Cohen Foundation for the grants they provided to help with the production of this publication. It is appropriate that a book giving details of sources of information on funding was itself able to attract financial support.

I would also like to acknowledge *Voluntary Forum Abstracts*, the existence of which made the task of compiling this bibliography much easier.

My thanks also to Maggie Barnes for her efficient typing of the manuscript.

Susan Bates *June 1986*

Introduction

This book is a guide to publications on the subject of the funding of the voluntary sector as a whole. In addition, its classified arrangement and subject index are designed to direct readers to sources of information on specific aspects of fund raising and grant aid.

What it includes

The first edition produced in 1981 included more or less every reference I could trace on the subject. The amount of literature available now is much greater. Consequently, I have been more selective for this edition. Even so, it includes twice as many references as the first one. To keep it to a manageable size, I have excluded more than 250 less important items. With a few exceptions, I have also excluded publications issued before 1981. This means that most of the publications listed in the first edition do not appear here unless they have themselves been updated. It is also limited to covering documents published in the United Kingdom.

In selecting material, one of my main considerations has been to include something on as wide a range of relevant topics as possible so that at least a starting point is given to someone looking for information on a particular subject. Where there are few publications on a topic, this may have resulted in the inclusion of some fairly insubstantial items.

Getting hold of publications

Journal articles. You may have easy access to the journal you want through work or other organisations you have contact with. If not, your local public library will be able to get hold of a copy of any article you want to see.

Books and pamphlets. Most of the books and pamphlets listed are still in print. Those issued by commercial publishers may be bought through booksellers. Many of the items included in the guide do not fall into this category and will have to be bought direct from the organisations which published them. To help you get hold of this type of publication, the 'Useful Addresses' section includes the addresses of these organisations.

If you don't want to buy an item or if it is out of print, then your local public library should be able to get hold of a copy for you to borrow.

A note on the accuracy of information

Inevitably, some of the information in the publications referred to will be out of date as the legal provisions affecting some fund-raising activities are regularly updated. The regulations on lotteries and gaming, for example, are frequently amended. And the changes affecting charities brought in by the 1986 budget mean that some of the information on the tax position of charities is no longer correct. Similarly, some of the information on sources of grant aid will become out of date as funding schemes are either withdrawn or amended and new ones introduced. To some extent it is possible to keep track of changes by reading the publications in Section 8 'Keeping up with new developments'. Other publications which should help with finding the most current information are *CANS* (Reference no. 292), *Legislation Monitoring Service for Charities* (Reference no. 287) and the *Craigmyle Guide to Charitable Giving* (Reference no. 272). These are issued periodically or regularly updated. If you need to check that the information you have is correct, or are looking for information or advice on specific aspects of funding, the organisations listed in the 'Useful Addresses' section may be able to help.

Bibliographic Entries

1 Philanthropy

1. Brittan, S.
'Hope, charity and welfare'
Financial Times, 22 December 1983

Samuel Brittan asks how we decide what proportion of our income to give to charity. The absolute morality of the matter is something we all have to determine for ourselves. One aspect of philanthropy, however, is within the realm of logical and political economy, i.e. 'interdependence effects' which arise from the fact that what we are prepared to give depends not only on our basic values but also on what we think other people will give. The reasoning behind different attitudes to giving is examined.

2. Institute of Economic Affairs
The Economics of Charity: Essays on the comparative economics and ethics of giving and selling, with applications to blood
The Institute of Economic Affairs, 1973, 197pp.

Part I consists of five essays on the ethics and economics of giving in general; Part II looks at the giving and selling of blood in particular

3. Mullin, R.
Present Alms: On the corruption of philanthropy
Phlogiston Publishing, 1980, 90pp.

Redmond Mullin explores the nature of charity and proposes a fundamental philosophy of philanthropy. He makes proposals for the improvement of non-profit organisations and of the quality and practice of giving.

4. Sugden, R.
Who Cares?: An economic and ethical analysis of private charity and the welfare state
The Institute of Economic Affairs, 1983, 45pp.

In *The Economics of Charity* Anthony Culyer proposed that the widespread desire to express care for other people explains the emergence of the welfare state. The basic idea is that people who are not themselves in need are willing to make gifts to those who are, but that each donor is willing to give only as part of an arrangement by which everyone gives. Hence, it is said, voluntary giving cannot

3

work and the desire to give can be satisfied only through a system of taxation and public spending: the welfare state. Robert Sugden rejects this proposition. He believes it conflicts with the evidence about voluntary giving and goes on to discuss alternative explanations of charity.

2 General References

This section includes publications which cover more than one subject and therefore do not fall easily into one of the other sections. There are very few books which attempt to cover the whole field but the most comprehensive ones are:

Fund Raising: A comprehensive handbook (Reference no. 5)

Fund Raising and Grant Aid: A practical and legal guide (Reference no. 10)

The Northern Ireland Fund Raising Handbook (Reference no. 9)

5. Blume, H.
Fund Raising: A comprehensive handbook
Routledge and Kegan Paul, 1977, 188pp.

This book covers the whole range of methods an organisation can use to raise money. It includes chapters on getting money from trusts, industry, central and local government; on covenants, legacies, house to house and street collections; on organising fund-raising functions, trading, mobilising other groups and using consultants. Some of the information is now out of date but much of the basic advice is still valid.

6. Charities Aid Foundation
Charities Aid Foundation 1984 Conference Report
CAF, 1985, 24pp.

The papers given at the conference include 'Why companies give' by Michael Brophy; 'What next after the House of Lords Select Committee Report on Parochial Charities' by Baroness Faithful and 'Organising the NSPCC's 100th anniversary appeal' by Giles Pegram.

7. Charities Aid Foundation
Coping with Change: Charity conference report, Drapers' Hall, London, 28 October 1982
Charities Aid Foundation, 1983, 7pp.

Charity must grow again if the new needs caused by a curious combination of unemployment, affluence, low growth and new technology are to be met. However, it is not clear where the money to support such a challenge is to come from. Although central government expenditure on the voluntary sector has increased in recent years, there is no overall government policy for it. Corporate responsibility within the voluntary sector is on the increase but still needs to be further extended. Contributions from government, companies, trusts and individuals could be maximised if a comprehensive tax concessionary system was introduced into the United Kingdom.

8. **Charity Commission**
Fund Raising by or for Charities (TP 20)
Charity Commission, 1984, 7pp.

This leaflet examines some of the considerations affecting fund raising for charities. The employment of professional fund raisers is examined including contracts, costs, and the image of the charity. The section on trading by and on behalf of charities considers trading as a means of raising funds, establishing a separate trading company and loans from charity. Finally the statutory provisions controlling various fund-raising methods are outlined, including street-collections, house to house collections, lotteries, and competitions and gaming.

9. **Courtney, R.**
The Northern Ireland Fund-Raising Handbook
Belfast Simon Community, 1983, 201pp.

This handbook is a practical introduction to fund raising for voluntary organisations in Northern Ireland. Part One looks at the preliminary process it is advisable an organisation goes through before starting to fund raise – looking at the organisation's aims and their financial implications, working out an appropriate fund-raising strategy. Part Two, the major part of the book, looks at sources of funds including government, trusts, industry, donations, collecting from the public, trading, sponsorship and organising fund-raising events.

10. **Darnborough, A. and Kinrade, D.**
Fundraising and Grant Aid: A practical and legal guide for charities and voluntary organisations
Woodhead-Faulkner, 1980, 160pp.

This guide includes chapters on: flag days; house to house collections; lotteries; bingo; pool betting; other gaming; tax reliefs; value-added tax; trading; sponsorship; waste collection; publicity; special appeals; consultants and sources of grant aid. Each chapter covers any relevant legislation.

11. **Davies, K.**
Community Groups' Information Pack
Hackney Community Action, 1983, 62pp.

Section three of this pack, 'Grants and other resources' looks at the whole process of grant-seeking. It starts with issues to consider before applying for a grant, who to apply to, deciding on strategy, writing the application, preparing the budget, lobbying potential funders, what to do if your project only gets part-funded and what happens after your grant has been approved. The other resources briefly looked at are student placements and secondment of paid workers.

6

12. The Directory of Social Change
Fund-Raising Notes for Capital Projects
The Directory of Social Change, 1984–1986, a series of 12 leaflets.
At the time of going to print, nine out of the series of 12 leaflets have been published.

Developing a strategy looks at how to decide where you should be looking for money.

Doing research is on how to undertake basic research into the need for the service you plan to provide to make your case for funding more compelling.

Drawing up a budget looks at how to plan your financial requirements for capital costs and your subsequent running costs.

Fund-raising sources looks at the main institutional sources of grants and donations: central government; local government and quangos; companies; grant-making trusts.

Planning an appeal is on how to organise an appeal for money for a capital project.

Planning a capital project looks at how to plan a building or landscape project, what is involved and what professional help you will require.

Raising money locally gives ideas for raising money from your supporters and the general public through donations, collections, lotteries and raffles, sponsored activities and fund-raising events.

Setting up looks at how to set up an organisation, draw up a constitution and apply for charitable status.

Writing an application gives advice on producing an effective grant application.

The three titles planned for publication in 1986 are:

Earning money. This will look at ways of earning money through charging for services or running small fund-raising activities.

Organising an event will look at what's involved in organising a successful fund-raising event.

Working with the MSC will be on how to work with the MSC Community Programme.

13. Farleigh, A.
Community Groups: A guide to funding
Brighton Council for Voluntary Service, 3rd edition, 1983, 68pp.

This guide is produced by a local organisation with the aim of helping other voluntary groups in the area find funding. Some of the information is of local interest only, but most of it is more generally relevant. Among the topics it covers are: raising money from local government, central government, trusts and industry; the benefits of charitable status; collecting money from the public; organising fund-raising social events.

14. **Greater London Council**
The Funding File Fact Pack
GLC, 1985, 42pp.

The Greater London Council produced this pack to help groups about to lose GLC support look for alternative funding. It describes the arrangements made to fill the gap left by the GLC's abolition and then goes on to give details of other sources of funding, mainly government departments and quangos.

15. **Investors Chronicle**
'Charities: An Investors Chronicle survey'
Investors Chronicle, annual
(Published in an issue of *Investors Chronicle* in Nov/Dec each year; the dates for the last few years' surveys are: 2 Dec. 1983, 23 Nov. 1984, 15 Nov. 1985)

The survey usually looks at trends in charitable giving based on information from the Charities Aid Foundation's *Charity Statistics* as well as picking out a few topics of current interest. For example, the 1983 survey looked at the most effective ways of giving to charity. The 1984 survey dealt with investment (including ethical investment), company giving and disaster relief. And the 1985 survey looked at the impact of the Ethiopian famine on aid charities, community involvement by companies, the Andrew Carnegie Trust on its 150th anniversary, housing associations, and investment.

16. **Islington Bus Company**
Fund Raising: A basic guide
Islington Bus Co., 1982, 29pp.

This guide looks at raising funds through organising events in the local community, government grants, grants from trusts and support from industry.

17. **Kirklees Association for Voluntary Organisations Funding**
Funding in the Voluntary Sector in Kirklees: Participation/partnership/
practice: report of a day conference at Dewsbury Town Hall on Tuesday 8th
March 1983
Kirklees Association for Voluntary Organisations Funding, 1983, 18pp.

Foster Murphy, Director of The Volunteer Centre, gave a talk on how to seek funding from non-statutory sources. Robin Hughes of the Voluntary Services Unit gave a personal view of statutory sources of funding. The local perspective was covered by Chris Mitchell of Voluntary Action Lewisham and John Bishop of Brighton Council for Voluntary Service. Participants talked about the funding situation for voluntary organisations in Kirklees and made suggestions for improving co-operation among voluntary groups and with the local authority.

18. Matthewson, A.
Funding Strategies Information Pack
Greater London Council Popular Planning Unit, 1986

This pack has separate sections on funding from local authorities, from district health authorities (joint finance), from central government, from trusts, general fund-raising techniques such as flag days and lotteries, fund raising from industry and funding for ethnic minority groups.

19. National Council for Voluntary Organisations Appeals Department and Information Department
Selective Bibliography of Fund Raising Books and Pamphlets
(NCVO Information Sheet, No. 17)
NCVO, revised edition, 1985, 5pp.

For anyone who is looking for a quick introduction to the main source of information on fund raising, this book list gives brief annotations for 22 of the most important books on the subject.

20. National Federation of Community Organisations
The Community Organisations Survival Kit
NFCO, 1982, 39pp.

This is a basic guide to ways of raising funds and saving money for community organisations and smaller locally based voluntary groups. It covers raising money in the local community, grants from charitable trusts, appeals to industry, fund raising and the law and saving money.

21. National Federation of Community Organisations
Information Sheets

Relevant sheets in this series are:
No. 10 Lotteries and gaming
No. 15 Rates
No. 20 Grant-aid procedure
No. 40 Applications to charitable trusts
No. 41 Money matters
No. 42 Organising a carnival or gala
No. 62 Community associations and value-added tax
No. 99 Bingo in community associations and village halls

22. Norton, M. and Blume, H.
Accounting and Financial Management for Charities
Directory of Social Change, 2nd edition, 1985, 104pp.

This includes a section on VAT concessions available to charities and one on costing a project for fund raising which is directed at people who are drawing up a grant application.

23. **Phillips, A. and Smith, K.**
Charitable Status: A practical handbook
Inter-Action Inprint, 2nd edition, 1982, 83pp.

Two chapters in this book, 'Charities and money giving' and 'Charities and tax relief' are relevant. The first covers charging for goods and services, occasional fund raising and trading. The second covers taxes payable by donors, halfway-house charities, taxes payable by charities and rate relief.

24. **Pinder, C.**
Community Start Up: How to start a community group and keep it going
National Extension College and National Federation of Community Organisations, 1985, 207pp.

Relevant sections cover the benefits of charitable status, applying for grants, grants from government, grants from trusts, and raising money from industry.

25. **Rowe, A.**
Changing Charity: A contribution to debate by a group of Conservatives
Conservative Political Centre, 1984, 49pp.

This pamphlet contains eight essays several of which relate to fund raising. Robert Key writes on fiscal concessions for charities. Andrew Rowe discusses anxieties about the use of charitable funds, including the proportion used for administration by charities and the proportion paid to professional fund raisers. A series of recommendations are made.

26. **Saint, D. P.**
'Is there life at the grass roots?'
Charity, **November 1985, Vol. 3, No. 1, pp. 11–12.**

Is the huge army of volunteers working to raise money for local causes in their own area now being overshadowed by the high powered professional? In an attempt to find out, a questionnaire was circulated to some leading charities. The author bases his article on their responses and on personal opinion. Direct giving to charity at a local level forms a fair proportion of the overall turnover – from 10% to 40% in the survey. Direct giving touches virtually every member of the public in one way or another. The types of activities it involves fall into four main areas: offering goods and services, sponsorship, gaming and what the author refers to as begging. He looks at the current situation and suggests changes he expects to see in the future.

27. **Scottish Community Education Council and Scottish Council for Community and Voluntary Organisations**
Funds For Your Project: A practical guide for community groups and voluntary organisations
SCEC and SCCVO, 1984, 58pp.

Funds For Your Project gives information on central government grants, local authority grants, grants from the European Economic Community, and applying to trusts. It also looks at help from businesses and includes some brief descriptions of how some organisations succeeded in getting grants and what they did with the money.

28. **Seed, P.**
One Day at a Time
Heinemann, 1979, 288pp.

This is an autobiographical account of the efforts of a cancer victim who launched an appeal and raised £1.5 million for the cause within three years.

29. **Semple, A.**
A–Z Fund Raising
Community Council for Suffolk, 1984, 55pp.

This booklet contains over 100 fund-raising ideas arranged in alphabetical order. They include appeal letters, advertising balloons, an auction of promises, waste paper collection and welly winging. A list of suppliers of some of the props of fund raising, such as lottery tickets, carnival equipment and balloons is given.

30. **Vogler, J.**
Recycling for Change: A handbook for fundraising by recycling
Christian Aid, 1985, 32pp.

Recycling waste to raise funds is an attractive idea. However, recycling schemes often fail because of inadequate planning or support. This pamphlet describes what's involved in setting up and running a recycling project – how to find out what waste is marketable, working out a budget to assess if your scheme will pay and the practicalities of collection, storage and delivery. The possibilities for different types of waste are looked at in turn and addresses are given of organisations offering help.

31. **Wales Council for Voluntary Action**
Supporting Voluntary Action in Wales: A review
WCVA, 1985, various paginations

Wales Council for Voluntary Action conducted a survey to review the extent and scope of voluntary activity in Wales. The completion of this review prompted WCVA to a re-appraisal of the support for voluntary action in Wales. Six separate groups were set up to consider different aspects. This publication gives the reports of all six groups including the one which considered the funding of voluntary organisations.

The charitable funds group's terms of reference were 'To consider the present position with regard to the availability of funds and other resources for voluntary action in Wales from statutory and non-statutory sources; the need for these resources as compared with other parts of the UK; the problems encountered with obtaining more resources of this kind; the possibility of viable new ideas regarding sources of funding; and to recommend to the Council what action might be taken'. The main recommendations of the group were that WCVA should

a) set up a Welsh Voluntary Trust

b) establish a national information and advice resource centre for voluntary organisations seeking funding support from non-statutory sources

c) seek the support of local authorities and other voluntary organisations to undertake a review of local charitable trusts throughout Wales.

32. Wiltshire Charities Information Bureau
Pennies from Heaven: A guide for Wiltshire voluntary organisations on sources of finance
Wiltshire Charities Information Bureau, 1984, leaflets in a folder

Pennies From Heaven is a pack of 19 fact sheets grouped into three categories. The first group gives information on a range of funding sources: trusts, local authorities, industry, Europe. The second group includes sheets on fund raising and the law, covenants and the benefits of charitable status. The last group gives information on funding for particular causes, such as for sport and recreation, for environmental or employment projects.

33. Woodd, C.
Crisis or Opportunity?: The funding of Westminster's voluntary organisations: the report of a survey by Voluntary Action Westminster
Voluntary Action Westminster, 1984, 40pp.

This report describes a study of the funding of voluntary organisations in the City of Westminster. It records and analyses the results of a detailed sample survey. The sources of statutory and non-statutory funds available to voluntary organisations in Westminster are reviewed. The problems that threaten the existence of many organisations are highlighted and recommendations are given on future policy.

3 Fund-raising Methods

3.1 Use of advertising, publicity and the media

34. Burnett, K.
Advertising by Charities
Directory of Social Change, 1986, 152pp.

This guide covers the main areas of promotion open to charities and voluntary organisations and is particularly aimed at those responsible for charity marketing and fund raising. The topics covered by the book are: why charities advertise; the tone and style of charity advertising; how to create successful advertising; how to evaluate your advertising; the use of direct mail; the use of inserts; how to write a successful appeal letter; how to obtain and present a radio or television appeal; poster advertising; how to raise money using the telephone.

Case studies of five successful charity campaigns are given.

35. Greaves, S.
'The hard sell for good causes'
The Times, 12 June 1985

Charities now employ advertising agencies and use pushy advertising campaigns in their appeals to the public for funds. Launching a country-wide campaign is expensive but the financial rewards are often worth it.

36. Kipling, R.
'Think before you advertise'
Voluntary Action, October 1985, Vol. 3, No. 8, p. 6

Ray Kipling thinks that some charities are wasting money on advertising campaigns to attract legacies. The value of advertising to solicitors, accountants and investment advisers is uncertain, yet the number of specialist handbooks aimed at these professional advisers is increasing. Charities need to be more professional in their approach and work out what the most appropriate form of advertising is for them. The author lists some of the factors a charity needs to consider in doing this. A table gives details of the distribution, number, frequency and advertising rates for some of the specialist publications which take this sort of advertising.

37. Kirby, J.
'Charity advertising'
Voluntary Action, November 1984, Vol. 2, No. 9, pp. 12–13

The author outlines the use of advertising agencies by charities to promote their causes and raise funds. In an advertising agency there will be a team of people who will handle a charity's advertising account and co-ordinate the campaign. Emotive appeals are now becoming less effective and promotional campaigns for medical charities rely more on factual information about the disease or handicap.

Some charities such as Dr Barnardo's do their own advertising. Smaller charities are in the dilemma of not having enough money to spend on advertising to become better known.

38. **Kirby, J. *et al.***
'Is this the way to market?'
Charity, September 1984, Vol. 1, No. 11, pp. 7–11, 14, 15

This is a series of four articles.

'Charity "ads": indulgence or a drive for minds' by Judy Kirby looks at the increased use by charities of advertising agencies.

'The need to know who wants to give' by Paul Riley finds that charities hold back from using research into motives and patterns of giving to help formulate their marketing policies.

'Hunger gives way to subtle selling' by Harold Simpton discusses how increased use of advertising and direct marketing by charities has improved public understanding and support for them.

'Styles will change, but we're nowhere near the limit' by Fred Morgan gives the views of four men on the future of charitable giving and how it might be increased, and in particular, their views on company giving and sponsorship.

39. **Leat, D.**
Charitable Fundraising by Means of Radio and Television: An exploratory study
The Volunteer Centre Media Project, 1981, 40pp.

Radio and television appeals are an important source of charitable funding. In 1979 more than £6.5 million was raised for charity by broadcast appeals. Two categories of issue are raised in the report: the first is concerned with the broad range of radio and television appeals and issues discussed include the amounts of money raised, the different types of appeal, and the controls exercised over appeals; the second category is described as 'charitable trustee' fund raising (eg, Thames Television's Telethon). The issues studied here were how this type of appeal is organised, the sources from which the money is raised and identifying the beneficiaries of this type of appeal.

40. **Leat, D.**
Charitable Fundraising by Means of Radio and Television: A Seminar, May 17 1982: report
The Volunteer Centre Media Project, 1982, 13pp.

This seminar, attended by people from charities and broadcasting organisations involved in radio and television fund-raising ventures, was called to discuss some of the issues raised in an earlier Media Project report (see entry no. 39). Issues discussed included the strengths and limitations of television fund raising, public accountability in local radio fund raising, the role of the Central Appeals

14

Advisory Committee, the selection of organisations and subjects for appeals and the allocation of funds raised from television and radio appeals.

41. **Leat, D.**
Help a London Child: A local radio charitable appeal
The Volunteer Centre Media Project, 1981, 6pp.
(Social Action and the Media; a series of case studies; No. 10)
The Help a London Child appeal has been run annually since 1975 and the amount of money raised has increased in each successive year. This case study describes the planning and preparation of the appeal, the event itself, coping with the response, allocating the funds and who benefits.

42. **McIntosh, D. and McIntosh, A.**
A Basic PR Guide for Charities
Directory of Social Change, 1985, 122pp.
This handbook gives advice to voluntary groups on public relations including advice on dealing with press, television and radio, developing campaigns, television and radio appeals and improving your organisation's public image.

43. **McIntosh, D. and McIntosh, A.**
Marketing: A guide for charities
Directory of Social Change, 1984, 158pp.
The authors believe it isn't sufficient for a charity to have a good cause and expect supporters to come knocking on its door. Even the most worthy of causes needs marketing.
Part I of the book summarises the points to consider when developing a marketing strategy, for example, why people give, targetting your appeals, promoting your cause. Part II looks at market research including, for example, how to find out more about your donors. Details of simple statistical procedures for evaluating the reliability of market research information are given.

44. **Mann, D.**
'Raising money through the BBC'
Trust News, **Spring 1983, pp.9–10**
This article provides a brief summary of how and when charitable appeals are made through broadcasting by the BBC. The BBC's aims and procedures for appeals are outlined including the roles of the Central Advisory Committee and the regional committees. There is a description of the methods by which applicants are selected and the conditions to be fulfilled by successful applicants. As well as regular appeals, emergency appeals are discussed and an assessment is made of the BBC annual appeal. The level of funds raised through regular appeals is examined including a league table of funds raised from 1980–1982.

45. *Media Project News*, September 1984, 22pp.

This issue of *Media Project News* looks at fund-raising opportunities on radio and television. It includes, among others, articles on the BBC's annual Children in Need appeal, on how BBC local radio stations contribute to charities, and on why there is no research for broadcast appeals.

46. **Mullin, R. (Chairman)**
Direct Response Advertising for Fund Raising Organisations: Proceedings of the IBIS conference held at the Bloomsbury Centre Hotel, 26 June 1978
IBIS Information Services Ltd, 1978, 150pp.

Direct response advertising is defined as 'an activity by which a seller directs his efforts to a qualified audience, using one or more media to solicit a response – by phone, mail or personal visit.' The conference looked at direct response advertising as a marketing device open to charities. It is suggested that it is in the interests of charities to acquire the skills and professionalism or to hire the services of those who have the skills, which are more usually associated with commercial product selling.

47. **Potts, P.**
'Collecting your conscience money?'
The Guardian, 28 September 1983

The author looks at advertisements used by charities in appealing to the public for donations. The images of vulnerable children keep the donations coming in but they aren't an accurate reflection of the people the charities are committed to. The advertisements perpetuate the role of charities as patrons and deny the rights of people with disabilities to have control over their public image. How many charities are prepared to discuss the contradictions in their work and risk revenue in favour of a concerted attack on prejudice?

48. **Pragnall, A. (Chairman)**
Report of the Working Party on Advertising by Charities on Independent Television and Independent Local Radio
Independent Broadcasting Authority, 1978, 48pp.

This is the report of a working party set up to look into whether there should be greater freedom for charities to buy advertising time on television and radio and, if so, under what conditions. Relaxation of the existing regulations was recommended. As yet, the recommendations have not been acted upon although the IBA is currently reviewing its regulations.

16

49. White, D.
'Switching off charity'
New Society, 20/27 December 1985, Vol. 74, No. 1199/1200, pp. 521-522

The Broadcasting Act 1981 prohibits any item on television or radio from giving publicity to the needs and objects of charity without the approval of the Independent Broadcasting Authority. Charities are allowed to advertise their events and activities over the air but the prohibition on publicising needs and objects means they cannot make a direct appeal for money. They can do this only through an appeal approved by an appeals advisory committee appointed jointly by the BBC and IBA.

Charities can earn more than £50,000 from a single appeal and more than £20 million has been raised in the 50 years the BBC has been broadcasting appeals. There have been attempts to get the prohibition lifted in the past and the issue has recently been raised again by the Independent Television Companies Association.

3.2 Organising fund-raising activities

50. Nicholl, K. (Editor)
Woman's Own Book of Fund Raising
Collins, 1986, 191pp.

The Woman's Own Book of Fund Raising is for groups who want to raise money, although individuals will be able to use some of the ideas. The first chapter describes different ways of raising funds, mainly through organising events such as coffee mornings and bazaars. The second chapter looks at fund raising and the law. Chapters 3 and 4 give ideas for things to cook and make to sell. The book ends with a checklist of points to consider when organising an event and a list of useful organisations.

51. Pearson, B.
The A to Z of Fund Raising: A comprehensive guide on money-making methods for Liberals and Social Democrats too
The Liberal Party, 1982, 67pp.

This is an alphabetical listing of fund-raising activities ranging from antiques, appeals and auctions to Xmas cards, zest and zeal. 104 different activities are described. Organisations providing services for fund raisers, e.g. hiring of fun fair equipment, printers of lottery tickets, are listed in an appendix.

52. Robinson, A.
Fund Raising A to Z: A manual for charitable and voluntary organisations
Kirkfield Publications, 1982, 64pp.

This is an alphabetical listing of fund-raising ideas and activities for charitable and voluntary organisations. There are over 50 entries which range from short notes on, for example, auctions, balloon races and Christmas hampers, to fuller descriptions of badge and candle making and selling, direct giving and sponsored events. A few suppliers of fund-raising stationery, badges etc. are listed.

53. **Saint, D.**
Group Fund Raising: A handbook for local organisers
Printforce, 1985, 81pp.

This guide offers advice to groups organising local fund-raising events. A range of activities is suggested which can be adapted to the needs of each individual organisation by making them simpler or more ambitious. Guidance is given on planning the events, budgeting, publicity, insurance and the law. Most importantly, the event needs to be enjoyable to attract people to participate and to encourage the organisers to make it successful.

54. **Sterrett, P.**
Fundraising Projects: 101 tried and proved projects
W. Foulsham & Co. Ltd, 1979, 120pp.

The projects described range from those suitable for small groups (e.g. how many peanuts does the jar hold?) to more ambitious schemes for larger groups. Suggestions range from the more usual, such as sponsored walks, to more original ideas, such as golf in the dark and wellie-throwing contests.

3.3 Trading

55. **Blume, H.**
Charity Christmas Cards: How to produce them, how to sell them, how to make money from them
Charities Advisory Trust, 1984, 91pp.

A quarter of all Christmas cards bought in Britain every year are sold in aid of charity. This guide gives practical help on the whole range of issues involved in the business: how to get the cards in the first place; handling orders; running a charity Christmas card shop; how much charities make from selling Christmas cards.

56. **Blume, H.**
The Charity Trading Handbook
Charities Advisory Trust, 1981, 234pp.

Trading in some form or another is an increasingly popular method of fund raising but it does not always have the profitable results hoped for. This handbook is designed to help organisations avoid making expensive mistakes. The topics on which advice is given include what products to sell, how to get them designed and manufactured, selling through thrift shops, selling by mail order and the law on charity trading.

18

57. National Council for Voluntary Organisations
Charity Shops (NCVO Information Sheet; No. 32)
NCVO, 1986, 6pp.

This information sheet explains what's involved in running a charity shop. It gives information on premises, management, using volunteers, getting hold of goods to sell and attracting customers.

58. Palmer, T.
'Business behind the birds'
Charity, January 1986, Vol. 3, No. 3, p. 23

Mail order trading is a major creator of image for a charity, but what does it produce in profit? This short article describes the size and operation of the Royal Society for the Protection of Birds' mail order business.

3.4 Investment

59. Charity Commission
The Charities Official Investment Fund: Explanatory memorandum
Charity Commission, 1971, 10pp.

This leaflet explains the purpose of the Charities Official Investment Fund, the advantages of participating in the scheme, and how it operates.

60. Charity Commission, The Official Custodian for Charities
Investment Management by Charity Trustees
Charity Commission, The Official Custodian for Charities, 1978, 12pp.

This pamphlet is a basic guide to the types of investment available to charities and the role of charity trustees in a charity's investment policy.

61. Ethical Investment Research and Information Service
Ethical and Social Investment
Ethical Investment Research and Information Service, Irregular

EIRIS's newsletter examines the ethics of particular types of investment and reports on 'alternative' investment opportunities.

62. Hibbert, A.
The Performance of Charitable Investments
Phillips and Drew, 1984, 4pp.

The author looks at the pattern of returns from the main forms of conventional investment available to UK charities over the period 1963–1983 to draw conclusions about the most advisable forms of investment for charity trustees to follow in the future.

63. **Lever, L.**
'Invest with care – and your ethics can stay intact'
Charity, January 1985, Vol. 2, No. 2, pp. 12–13

This article looks at the issues surrounding ethical investment. One of the obstacles to a charity wanting to pursue an ethical investment policy is the obligation charity trustees are under to protect the charity's property. If pursuing an ethical investment policy results in lower returns, then the trustees may be seen as failing in this duty.

64. **MacLachlan, R.**
'First catch your stockbroker'
Voluntary Action, February 1985, Vol. 3, No. 1, pp. 12–13

This article outlines the legal framework of charity investment based on the 1961 Trustee Investments Act. Two major options for charity investment are discussed: government stocks and commercial shares. The work of the Official Custodian for Charities, including its Charities Official Investment Fund, is mentioned.

65. **MacLachlan, R.**
'Profits – and principles too'
Voluntary Action, April 1985, Vol. 3, No. 3, pp. 11

Under the 1961 Trustee Investments Act, charities are required to choose investments which produce the maximum financial benefit. But does this necessarily mean a charity cannot have an ethical investment policy? The article concludes that it is possible for charities to use ethical criteria for deciding where to invest their money.

66. **Norton, M.**
Investment of Charity Funds
Directory of Social Change and Charities Aid Foundation, 1985, 85pp.

Investment of Charity Funds is written primarily for charity trustees and for members of staff with responsibility for the financial affairs of their organisation. It looks at the options available for the investment of short-term money, medium-term money and long-term investment. Other issues discussed are: taxation on interest and dividends; comparing interest rates; the requirements of the Trustee Investments Act; and the performance of charitable investments.

67. **Young Friends Central Committee**
Alternative Investment: Opportunities for Quakers and others
Young Friends Central Committee, 2nd edition, 1984, 63pp.

This booklet aims to encourage Quakers (and others) to invest in areas which Quakers positively wish to support. The meaning of alternative investment is explained and the reasons for choosing this type of investment. The legal requirements and obligations on trustees in relation to investment are covered. Details of 30 alternative investments are given.

3.5 Donations

68. **Ashworth, M.**
'Individual donations to charity'
Charity Statistics, 1982/83, pp. 14–15

This article gives some preliminary analysis of survey information on individual charitable donations collected from 3,550 households for the *Family Expenditure Survey*. Tables show details of donations in relation to different variables: income of household, age of head of household and occupation of head of household.

69. **Baker, N.**
'The charity boom'
The Times Educational Supplement, 6 July 1984, p. 8

Charitable fund raising in schools has reached multi-million pound proportions, highlighting the complex moral issues involved in such activities and the way they are carried out. Nick Baker examines how three organisations – Help the Aged, the National Society for the Prevention of Cruelty to Children and the Young Men's Christian Association – approach fund raising in schools.

70. **Bridge, T.**
Donations to Charity: An analysis of money given by secondary schools in Humberside
Community Council of Humberside, Charities Information Bureau, 1984, 11pp.

In December 1983 a questionnaire was sent from the Charities Information Bureau of Humberside through the Education Department to all 64 secondary schools in Humberside to discover the kind and amount of giving to charity which takes place. This pamphlet provides a summary of the responses. It covers the amounts of money donated, who receives the money, and the policy schools had on charitable giving.

71. **Charities Aid Foundation**
Giving to Charity: Higher rate tax relief
CAF, 1986, Leaflet

This leaflet explains the benefits of giving by covenant for people who pay above the basic rate of income tax.

72. **Charities Aid Foundation**
   Legacies to Charity
   CAF, (no date), Leaflet

   This leaflet explains how to leave money to charity and how the services of the Charities Aid Foundation can help.

73. **Charities Aid Foundation**
   Personal Charitable Giving
   CAF, 1985, 16pp.

   This pamphlet explains the Charities Aid Foundation's discretionary covenant service for donations to charity by individuals.

74. **Fielding, N.**
   'Flag raising'
   New Society, 21 February 1986, *Voluntary Action Supplement*, p.iii

   Are charity flag days worth the effort? The biggest flag day, the poppy appeal organised by the Royal British Legion, raised £7.4 million in 1985. But some organisations don't think flag days are worth the effort. The Spastics Society has found more productive ways of raising money. However, even though the overall proportion of charity income from fund raising and donations dropped by 40 per cent between 1976–81, flag day income is holding its own. The key to raising money is the number of people on the streets. There are also spin-offs: publicity for the organisation and contact with the public.

75. **Hadley, J.**
   'Charity in the classroom'
   Voluntary Action, October 1984, Vol. 2, No. 8, pp. 7–8

   There is a growing concern about the methods used by some charities to raise cash using school children through, for example, sponsored swims. Some charities now raise large sums of money this way; Help the Aged raised £2 million in 1982. Particular concern has been expressed about the competitive element of fund raising by sponsorship. A code of conduct for fund raising in schools is being prepared by the Institute of Charity Fundraising Managers.

76. **Mintel Market Intelligence**
   'Charities'
   MINTEL Market Intelligence, October 1983, pp. 29–41

   The first part of this article is an analysis of the 'charity market' largely based on an analysis of the Charities Aid Foundation 'Charity Statistics'. The second part is on individuals' donations to charity based on Mintel commissioned consumer research carried out by British Market Research Bureau with a sample of 1,028 adults in June 1983. In the previous year, 54 per cent had given money to cancer research, 53 per cent to the poppy appeal, 35 per cent to the Royal National Lifeboat Institution and 32 per cent to childrens' charities. Women and older people are more likely to give as are those in the upper income groups. Results of questions on public attitudes to charity are also reported.

77. **Norton, M.**
Leaving Money to Charity
Directory of Social Change, 1983, 60pp.

The aim of this booklet is to encourage people to leave money to charity and to give practical guidance on how to go about it. It is also expected to help charities answer questions from their supporters when asked by the charity to leave them a legacy.

The guide looks at: making a will; working out how much you're worth and who you want to leave your money to; how to leave money to charity; organising charitable bequests; the types of legacy available; how to choose a charity; and the tax position. Sample forms of wording for bequests to charity are given.

78. **Norton, M.**
Legacies: A practical guide for charities
Directory of Social Change, 1983, 153pp.

Legacies are an important source of income for charities. Approximately £260 million is left to charity by people in their wills each year, yet it is a source of funds which many charities ignore. This book looks at the importance of legacy income to charities; it gives statistics on the amount of money charities are currently getting in the form of legacies and which charities are receiving this money. It then goes on to give advice on: how a charity can increase its income from legacies; advertising for legacy income; memorials as a source of income; the legal aspects of leaving money to charity; and capital transfer tax. Suggested wording for legacies and codicils are included.

79. **Saint, D.**
'Put a slot in it!'
Charity, March 1986, Vol. 3, No. 5, pp. 14–15

David Saint looks at collecting money from the public using collecting boxes in static positions rather than by house to house and street collections. The article talks about sites for collecting boxes, their design and new developments such as covering some of the costs with sponsorship from firms. Although the initial costs can be quite high, they can be worthwhile for even a small charity as long as it has the resources to place the boxes and visit sites regularly to empty them. And there are benefits over and above the straight financial gains.

80. Vickers, J.
'Collecting for charity'
Local Government Chronicle, 3 July 1981, No. 5956, pp. 688–689

This article gives an explanation of the responsibilities of local authorities for issuing licences for house to house and street collections, and also covers the role of the police in granting certificates of exemption.

81. Which?
'Giving to charity'
Which? September 1984, pp. 390–393

Which? looks at what a charity is and the best ways individuals can give to charities. Tables based on returns of a questionnaire to 2,000 *Which?* readers show the average amounts each respondent gave to charity in 1983, how they gave to charity (for example, through street collections, covenants etc) and the most popular charities.

82. Will To Charity Ltd
Charities and Legacy Fund Raising
Will To Charity Ltd, 1983, 11pp.

This pamphlet contains four articles: 'Do charities need legacies?'; 'Where legacies fit in fund raising'; 'Getting "in" on the legacy scene'; and 'Advertising for legacy income'.

3.6 Payroll giving

83. FitzHerbert, L.
The Community Fund: A new approach to supporting voluntary activity: report of the United Way Feasibility Study
United Way Feasibility Study, 1983, 44pp.

This is the report of a study to look at the feasibility of establishing payroll deduction schemes in Britain. It explores whether, and how, a systematic approach could be taken to increasing voluntary contributions and personal involvement through the payroll deduction method. The principles, potential benefits and operation of Community Funds are described. What's involved in organising a Community Fund, including copies of sample documents needed, is also covered.

84. Freeman, F. C.
The SUVOC Application: Why and how to develop substantial new resources for the voluntary sector through workers' payroll giving
United Way of Merseyside (National Division), 2nd edition, 1983, 306pp.

The SUVOC Application (SUVOC stands for Society of United Voluntary Organisations within Community) is about a method of providing new resources for the voluntary sector through workers' payroll giving. The author claims that it is designed to improve the social, economic and personal health of the nation through increased free-will giving of services and monetary aid. The author considers why this is a worthy and necessary objective and outlines, with administrative details, one possible democratic procedure whereby this objective could be realised.

85. **O'Sullivan, S.**
'Paypacket charity'
Voluntary Action, June 1985, Vol. 3, No. 5, pp. 10–11

The York Community Fund is one of six pilot schemes around the country being promoted by a charity called United Funds. The scheme has about 370 people from different employers in York who regularly covenant a small proportion of their wages to charity. In York £28,000 has been pledged to charity over the next four years.

3.7 Links with industry

86. **Berkshire Charities Combined Fundraising Association**
The Berkshire Coffer: A report on the activities of the Berkshire Charities Combined Fundraising Association
Berkshire Charities Combined Fundraising Association, 1984, 20pp.

The Berkshire Charities Combined Fundraising Association (CoFA) was established in 1982 with the object of helping voluntary organisations in the county raise money to maintain and develop their work. In its promotion of fund-raising events CoFA seeks the sponsorship of commercial and industrial enterprises with business interests in the county. In its first year, CoFA raised £21,000 with a total of nine sponsorships.

87. **British Institute of Management**
Corporate Charitable Giving
BIM, 1982, 6pp.

This checklist, prepared in conjunction with the Charities Aid Foundation, highlights the questions companies should ask when reviewing their policy and practice towards charities. Fifty-five questions cover: overall policy; level of giving; employee involvement; implementation; selecting recipients; follow up; public relations; and taxation.

88. **Business in the Community**
Business in the Community: A guide to action
BIC, 1984, 12pp.

Business in the Community helps industry and professionals contribute to the community. There is an emphasis on local action in the areas where the firms operate. It is a partnership of business and enterprise, the statutory and voluntary sectors, and private institutions. Business can help the community in a number of ways; by contributing financially, secondment of staff centrally and to local projects, encouraging employees to participate in local community action, and involvement in pilot and innovatory schemes. This involvement can benefit all: it enhances the company and the community, helps employees, and promotes better recruitment.

89. **Clutterbuck, D.**
How to be a Good Corporate Citizen: A manager's guide to making social responsibility work and pay
McGraw-Hill, 1981, 294pp.

Chapter 2, 'Corporate giving' discusses the policies of various companies on giving to charities. Chapter 3, 'A helping hand' talks about the secondment of employees to charities.

90. **Cowton, C.**
'Charities and company giving: some reflections'
Charity Statistics, 1982/83, pp. 16–19

This article discusses the relationship between companies as donors and charities as recipients of funds. Problems in the relationship are highlighted. Many of the problems seem to be rooted in mutual ignorance and could be alleviated by the provision and better use of information on both sides. Better information would improve understanding and increase the flow of funds.

(See also ref no. 91)

91. **Cowton, C.**
'Company charitable giving: practice and disclosure'
Charity Statistics, 1981/82, pp. 54–56

This article reports on the progress of a research project into the practice and disclosure of corporate giving. The aim of the project is to investigate the effect of the requirement to disclose information on charitable giving by discovering who uses the information and whether company donations would change if the requirement were abolished.

(See also ref. no. 90)

92. **Davies, R.**
'Company cash and a whole lot more'
Voluntary Action, October 1984, Vol. 2, No. 8, p. 14

Companies are taking a more practical and active interest in the work of voluntary organisations rather than passively waiting for begging letters. Non-cash resources such as old office equipment, 'waste' products such as timber and cloth, making meeting rooms, printing and training facilities available, secondment of personnel and cash donations are among the sorts of help offered. Advice on how to tap this desire to help is offered.

93. **Davies, R.**
How Voluntary Organisations Can Benefit From Business (NCVO Information Sheet; No. 30)
National Council for Voluntary Organisations, 1985, 4pp.

This information sheet is an initial guide for voluntary organisations wanting to build up practical links with the business sector. The resources companies can offer fall into three categories: 1. Non-cash resources, such as use of office equipment and printing facilities; 2. Personnel, including secondment of staff or employee involvement as volunteers; 3. Cash, including donations and employee community funds. A strategy for developing contacts and making approaches to the business community is suggested.

94. **Davies, R.**
'Working with voluntary organisations'
Business in the Community, April 1984, Supplement, 6pp.

This BIC supplement describes just a few examples of business involvement with the voluntary sector in community initiatives. The involvement of Levi Strauss and Co, Johnson Wax, Unilever and Marks and Spencer is outlined. Some enterprise agencies are working with the voluntary sector. A number of projects for the unemployed are described. Businesses are advised how to make contact with the voluntary sector and help in community initiatives.

95. **Erlichman, J.**
'Charities count mighty companies' mite'
The Guardian, 30 November 1983

Only one per cent of voluntary contributions received by charities is donated by companies. In the United States, companies are at least five times more generous in their cash donations. Sara Morrison, director of GEC, believes firms in the UK offer less in voluntary contributions because they pay so heavily through corporation tax to support the welfare state. Companies in the UK give a disproportionate share of their donations to arts charities like the Royal Opera House, and less to the 'caring' charities which help the sick, poor and disabled. Charities are often amateurish in their approach to companies and need to be more business-like.

96. **Erlichman, J.**
'A kind of giving'
Voluntary Action, March 1984, Vol. 2, No. 2, pp.14–15

Business in the Community estimates that there may be as many as 1,500 people
whose companies have seconded them on full salary to work in voluntary
organisations, but this number is minute compared with the number in the
United States. In the last ten years BIC and Action Resource Centre have sought
to promote greater business involvement in the voluntary sector, but motives in
boardrooms are mixed with some companies using secondment as a way of
getting rid of redundant old staff. A few companies, for example Marks &
Spencer, encourage young and middle-aged staff to go on secondment in the
voluntary sector. Secondment is shown to have lasting benefits to companies,
employees and the community.

97. **Grant, S. *et al.***
'Giving people: it ought to do good all round'
Charity, March 1985, Vol. 2, No. 5, pp.11–13, 15

Secondment is an arrangement whereby an employee is loaned without loss of
pay to a project either inside or outside the company. Everyone involved benefits.
The company enhances its philanthropic image; the employee gains valuable
experience outside his or her normal job; and the charity gains free use of an extra
member of staff with skills needed by the organisation. The main organisations
working to arrange secondment opportunities are the Action Resource Centre
and Business in the Community. Several secondees give their accounts of the
experience.

98. **Head, V.**
Sponsorship: The newest marketing skill
Woodhead-Faulkner, 1981, 116pp.

The author begins by defining sponsorship and tracing its history and development. He looks at the opportunities for sponsorship in the two areas in which it is
most often used – sport and the arts. The final chapters give advice to companies
considering sponsorship on identifying its objectives, choosing and servicing a
sponsorship. This includes advice for organisations seeking sponsorship on how
to woo a potential sponsor.

99. **Hicks, C.**
'Hambro handouts'
Voluntary Action, Autumn 1983, No. 16, pp. 8–9

Hambro Life based in Swindon since 1971, one of the country's largest life
assurance companies, has given grants of almost £750,000 for Swindon's community and voluntary projects. Hambro gives about £150,000 a year. Grants are
made to small self-help groups, such as the Stroke Support Group, and larger

well established groups, such as Age Concern and the Red Cross. Other schemes include unemployed and young offenders' centres. The only criterion for a grant is that money should go towards 'social welfare'. Local voluntary bodies are very pleased but there is a criticism: does Hambro let the statutory bodies off the hook by funding services that are their responsibility?

100. **Infield, G. M. *et al.***
'Planned giving:
1. **Ford Motor Company Limited and Ford of Britain Trust**
2. **The Rank Foundation**
3. **Levi Strauss & Co. Limited**
4. **Marks & Spencer P.L.C.'**
Charity, May 1984, Vol. 1, No. 7, pp.9–10, 12

Increasingly companies involved in giving to charity are developing well thought-out policies and taking the initiative instead of simply responding to requests for money from charities. Here, the policies of four companies are described.

101. **Kidd, H.**
Companies, Charity and Tax: USA and UK: Three essays
Charities Aid Foundation, 1985, 46pp.

The first of the three essays looks at how corporate giving works in the USA and why American companies give more than their British counterparts. The second essay compares charity and taxation in the two countries. The final essay looks at how three British companies are involved in charitable activity.

102. **Kirkham, C.**
Crossover
1. *From company to community*
2. *Why Crossover?*
3. *Voluntary organisations*
4. *Introducing Crossover*
5. *Starting up Crossover*
6. *Pulling it all together*
The Volunteer Centre, 1985, six pamphlets in a folder

The Crossover Project aims to ease the retirement transition for employees by introducing them to voluntary work before they retire. To achieve this, the project asks employers to start Crossover schemes by granting paid release from work for employees nearing retirement. This pack of pamphlets explains how the scheme works to companies who may be interested in getting involved.

29

103. **Kirkham, C. and Whates, P.**
'Taking a wider view: the company at work in the community'
Involve, May 1985, No. 43, pp.8–11
and
'The company at work in the community – Part two'
Involve, July 1985, No. 44, pp.10–11
and
'The company at work in the community – Part three'
Involve, December 1985, No. 47, pp.4–6

This series of articles looks at the wide variety of ways in which companies are acting to put the philosophy of corporate social responsibility into practice. Encouraging fund raising for voluntary organisations by employees, establishing payroll deduction schemes and arranging secondments of staff to voluntary organisations are some of the examples given.

104. **Knox, J. and Ashworth, M.**
An Introduction to Corporate Philanthropy
British Institute of Management and Charities Aid Foundation, 1985, 30pp.

Corporate philanthropy can take many forms. Companies give money and make matching grants, donate goods, services and facilities, and support their employees in voluntary activities and secondments. In order to obtain maximum effect all these efforts should be integrated, and decisions made according to clearly stated objectives which are part of corporate policy. Corporate philanthropy must be subject to the same standards of management required in normal company operations. This review, designed for company executives, describes a variety of philanthropic activities available to companies, and proposes organisational and management arrangements for operating corporate grant efforts. A general summary of relevant tax regulations is included.

105. **Logan, D.**
'Levi's and local initiatives'
Initiatives, August 1983, No. 6, pp.7–9

The manager of Community Affairs of the Northern Europe Division of Levi Strauss describes his company's charitable giving programme which focuses on those areas where the firm is an employer. Instead of attempting to service the needs of charities and the voluntary sector at the national level, there is a system of grants which allows the workforce in each factory to become involved in managing a local community grants policy.

106. **McIntosh, D.**
'Chainstore charity'
Voluntary Action, May 1984, Vol. 2, No. 4, pp.10–11

Joint promotions between charities and manufacturers in which charities gain funds and manufacturers increase sales and good public image are now familiar. Joint promotions between retailers and charities are a recent development. Charities are advised to approach retailers and co-operate with them in joint promotion ventures. Save the Children has run successful joint promotions with Fine Fare and International Stores, Age Concern with Tesco, various charities with Safeway and the Scottish Society for the Prevention of Cruelty to Children with the Scottish Midland Co-op. Problems are also described and the need for charities to be business-like in their methods emphasised.

107. **Mauksch, M.**
Corporate Voluntary Contributions in Europe
New York, The Conference Board, 1982, 41pp.

This reports on a survey of corporate philanthropy in eight European countries, including the United Kingdom. Only 3 per cent of questionnaires mailed were returned, so conclusions are tentative.

108. **Norton, M.**
A Guide to Company Giving
Directory of Social Change, 1984, 152pp.
(NB A new edition is due to be published in September 1986)

Companies are an important source of support for charities. Michael Norton estimates company support for charity to be £132.5 million. This includes donations, sponsorship, advertising, joint promotions and secondments but not gifts in kind.

The bulk of *A Guide to Company Giving* is taken up with information on the top 1,000 company donors. There are two listings of these 1,000 companies, first ranked by size of donation and then listed alphabetically with statistical information on the company. The donations policies of the 135 largest donors are also given.

The book also deals with tax and company donations, how to do an appeal to companies, company trusts, secondment of staff, sponsorship and joint promotions.

109. **Norton, M.**
Industrial Sponsorship and Joint Promotions
Directory of Social Change, 1981, 116pp.

This is a companion guide to *Raising Money From Industry (see ref. No. 110)*. It describes two forms of commercial activity which can be used by charities as a means of raising money – sponsorship and joint promotions. It looks at the opportunities and dangers of sponsorship and how to go about getting sponsorship at both national and local levels. An explanation of how joint promotions work is given along with case studies from UNICEF and the World Wildlife Fund on how they used joint promotions to raise money.

110. **Norton, M.**
Raising Money from Industry
Directory of Social Change, 1981, 116pp.

Raising Money from Industry looks at the motivations for company giving and the forms it takes. Advice on how to decide which firms to approach and how to go about it is given. There are contributions from people working in industry explaining their company's policy on giving to charity. Also discussed are employee or payroll giving, and non-monetary methods of giving to charity through secondment of staff, provision of advice on management and marketing skills and gifts in kind.

111. **United Biscuits**
UB in the Community: Illustrating some of the ways United Biscuits works with local communities
United Biscuits, 1984, 16pp.

United Biscuits subscribes to the philosophy that industry has a responsibility to be more actively involved in community initiatives. This collection of articles from the company's journal shows a variety of projects in which it has been involved. These include advisory services to small businesses and projects to help unemployed young people. The company also contributes in cash and kind to community development projects and has seconded staff through the Action Resource Centre's schemes. It also encourages its staff to get involved in fund raising for community projects.

3.8 Community trusts

112. **Charities Aid Foundation**
'Community trusts are more than "funnels" '
Charity, June 1984, Vol. 1, No. 8, p. 4

At the first formal meeting of Community Trusts in this country a description of common characteristics was established: they are 'organisations set up under a Board of Trustees, using several sources of income to cater for a wide variety of needs (not just through funding) in a defined community'. In addition to the problems encountered by all grant-seeking charities, Community Trusts are under the extra pressure to persuade potential donors and supporters that they are the ideal focal point for local funding. The results of a Charities Aid Foundation questionnaire to 40 Community Trusts, to which only 10 replied, are discussed.

113. **Charities Aid Foundation**
The Report of a Working Party Set up to Consider the Concept of Community Trusts in the United Kingdom
CAF, 1984, 25pp.

The working party sees 'the creation of community trusts as something which, in the longer term, might help to promote partnership between statutory, private and voluntary sectors, help generate money, and channel it to the points where it can be most effective in meeting local community needs, especially those not reached by existing sources of funding.'

The report explains the concept of community trusts, their relevance to the community, and the process involved in setting one up. It recommends that a number of pilot trusts be set up to demonstrate whether or not they are viable and effective.

114. **Northern Ireland Voluntary Trust**
Annual Reports, 1979/80 onwards

The establishment of this Trust is described as an unique attempt to provide funds for voluntary groups in Northern Ireland. It was set up in 1979 with an initial grant of £500,000 on the initiative of the government which saw the need for an independent agency to provide financial support and encouragement to voluntary and community groups, particularly those whose work is involved with tackling social problems. The Trust raises money from private sources and has a matching grant arrangement with the Department of Health and Social Services whereby for each £1 donated to the Trust's capital fund, the DHSS will give £1. The annual reports give details of the Trust's services and the organisations funded.

115. **South Yorkshire Charity Information Service Trust**
A Local Voluntary Trust in South Yorkshire
South Yorkshire Charity Information Service Trust, 1984, 7pp.

This paper explores the idea of setting up a local voluntary trust in South Yorkshire to help meet contemporary community needs. The trust's remit would be community wide and its funds would be sought from the community itself: from industry, commerce, legacies, individuals and some statutory support. The trust would build a pool of capital whose income would be distributed to foster and strengthen the locality's 'community spirit' and provide a spur for new development. In the United States, there are more than 250 community trusts operating, but as yet, the only one of any significance in the UK is the Northern Ireland Voluntary Trust *(see ref. No. 114)*.

The main steps to form and operate a community trust are outlined and structural and financial implications explained. Appendices contain a note on community trusts in the USA and details of the Northern Ireland Voluntary Trust.

116. **Wales Council for Voluntary Action**
'Funding voluntary action in Wales: the case for a Welsh voluntary trust'
Network Wales, Jan/Feb 1986, No. 28, pp. 10–11

Welsh voluntary organisations receive a disproportionately small amount of funding from central government and charitable sources in comparison to their counterparts in other areas of the United Kingdom. This article looks at the proposal to establish a Welsh voluntary trust as a means of providing new resources for the voluntary sector in Wales.

3.9 Using consultants

117. **MacLachlan, R.**
'An A–Z of fundraising firms'
Voluntary Action, Autumn 1983, No. 16, pp. 10–11

Based on returns from a questionnaire sent to 26 firms, the services and records of 18 fundraising consultants are compared. A table gives details for each firm of its form of business, years in operation, number of consultants, services offered, information from the firms' records over the last three years including average fee, and information on the terms of contracts offered by the firm. The names, addresses and phone numbers for each firm are also given.

118. **MacLachlan, R.**
'Raising funds – and hackles too'
Voluntary Action, Winter 1982, No. 13, pp. 11–12

Fund-raising consultants have, as a profession, a poor public image. Yet the number of consultants is growing so they must be answering a practical need. At a rough estimate, there are 150 people making their living selling advice to charities. This article looks at the different methods of charging for their services used by consultants and at the need for some form of regulation.

119. **Richards, A. L.**
'Fund-raising?: not when it costs 79p in every £1'
Charity, May 1984, Vol. 1, No. 7, pp. 14–15

A.L. Richards, a member of the Institute of Charity Fund Raising Managers, describes the role of a professional fund-raising consultancy. He argues that charities need to know how to raise funds efficiently and profitably. Charities require standardised and accurate accounts, so that their managers can know whether they are making the most of their limited resources to raise funds.

120. Scarlet, I.
'A potential for abuse?'
Voluntary Action, July 1985, Vol. 3, No. 6, pp. 12–13

The press has recently reported instances of professional fund raisers working for charities but pocketing most of the money raised for themselves. In 1983 four men involved in commercial fund raising for a registered charity called Children With Cancer were charged with conspiring to obtain money by deception. All four men were acquitted 18 months later. Iain Scarlet goes into the facts of the case and reasons why it wasn't possible to convict the men under the law as it stands.

4 Grant Aid

4.1 Trusts

121. Acquaah, E. K.
Knowledge is Money?: An evaluation of the usefulness of information provided by the West Yorkshire Charities Information Bureau to voluntary groups
West Yorkshire Charities Information Bureau, 1986, 43pp.

The West Yorkshire Charities Information Bureau, which gives advice on funding, mainly trust funding, wanted to find out what happened to the information it gave and how organisations perceived that information. The results of a study arranged by the bureau show it provides a very cost effective service. Organisations contacting the bureau obtained grants which otherwise would probably not have gone to groups in West Yorkshire. The 62 organisations taking part in the survey raised £172,954 between them and of this, £62,000 was from sources they had not known about before contacting WYCIB.

122. Courtney, R.
Fundraising Through Trusts
Northern Ireland Council for Voluntary Action, 1985, 98pp.

The first part of this book gives advice on how to decide which trusts to approach, how to write the application and what to expect in reply . The second part is a directory of 58 trusts based in Northern Ireland, or based outside but known to give grants to projects in Northern Ireland.

123. Craven, F.
'Bridging the gap between the grant givers and grant seekers'
Voluntary Action, Winter 1983, No. 17, p. 23

This article describes the origins and work of charity information bureaux. At the time of writing, there were five operating in England. The aim of such bodies is to make fund raising more efficient by assisting grant seekers to find appropriate grant givers. They are also taking an interest in other types of fund raising, such as payroll deductions and income creating schemes such as the production of charity Christmas cards.

124. FitzHerbert, L.
A Guide to the Major Grant-Making Trusts
Directory of Social Change, 1986, 140pp.

This guide provides information on the grant-making policies and practices of over 200 major trusts which between them make grants of more than £140 million a year. The main reason for producing this detailed guide is to help grant-seeking organisations make more informed choices about which trusts it is worthwhile applying to. Appendices on other sources of information and advice look at the Charity Commission Register of Charities, charity information bureaux and councils for voluntary service and at using the *Directory of Grant-Making Trusts*. There is also advice on how to approach a trust.

125. **Goodenough, S.**
The Greatest Good Fortune: Andrew Carnegie's gift for today
Macdonald Publishers, 1985, 290pp.

Andrew Carnegie used his vast fortune to endow numerous trusts to ensure his money would be well spent after his death. This account of the Carnegie trusts looks at how they have gone about their job, how they see their roles today and the impact of their work on past and present society.

126. **Hodson, H. V.**
The International Foundation Directory
Europa Publications, 3rd edition, 1983, 401pp.

This directory lists 705 international trusts and foundations and large national foundations which have had an international impact. The fields in which the trusts operate range from science and medicine to social welfare, education, the arts, aid to developing countries and international relations. The entry for each organisation gives its name, address, purpose and information on its finances, activities and officers. Entries are arranged by country but there is an alphabetical index and a listing of the foundations under broad subject headings.

127. **Johnson, W.**
'The role of grant making trusts today'
Trust News, **Autumn, 1985, No. 10, pp. 4–6**

Wallis Johnson believes that the greater exposure to the public that trusts have received in recent years is beneficial. This increased exposure will lead to more applications coming in and hopefully to a sharpening of the criteria for evaluating them.

Some trusts are tightly controlled by their trust deed, but where this allows trustees a wide discretion in the purposes for which the money can be used, what role should they attempt to play? The author believes that a major role for them is to foster innovation. He also outlines a further six specific roles:
experimenting with new ways of delivering services
keeping the definition of charity up to date
supporting minority interests
supporting matters of conscience
strengthening the voluntary sector
influencing government policies.

128. **Lazenby, L. and Nayler, H.**
A Merseyside Directory of Grant-Making Trusts
Liverpool Council for Voluntary Service and The John Moores Foundation,
1985, no pagination

This directory lists 128 trusts and other grant-making bodies which are based in Merseyside and/or give preference to applications from Merseyside. In total, these trusts distribute over £4.5 million annually. The directory has two subject indexes, one listing trusts which fund organisations, one listing trusts which fund individuals. There is also a geographical index, and the main section which gives information on the trusts themselves.

129. **MacLachlan, R.**
'Charitable trusts – time for a shake up'
Voluntary Action, October 1985, Vol. 3, No. 8, pp. 10–11

Collecting information on how trusts spend their money is very difficult, so any attempt to assess the responsiveness of trusts to changing needs must be tentative. But there are grounds for believing a general shake-up of methods and attitudes is needed. Publicising their interests and thus encouraging applications from people working 'in the front line' is one way to keep in touch. But many trusts give the impression of deliberately discouraging public interest. The composition of boards of trustees, predominantly white, male, middle class and middle aged, can lead to a built-in bias. One suggestion to keep trusts in touch with reality is that they should have a 'public trustee', with the appointment made by the local authority.

130. **MacLachlan, R.**
'How to impress a charitable trust'
Voluntary Action, November 1985, Vol. 3, No. 9, pp. 12–13

This article advises on how to improve your chances of getting money from a trust. Doing the initial research thoroughly, trying local trusts, providing all the basic information needed by the trust to assess your application are among the tips given.

131. **MacLachlan, R.**
'The secret world of charitable trusts'
Voluntary Action, September 1985, Vol. 3, No. 7, pp. 14–15

This first article in a series of three looks at the origins of charitable trusts in Britain.
(See ref. nos 129 and 130 for the other two articles in the series.)

132. **MacLachlan, R.**
'Tapping trusts'
New Society, 18 October 1985, Vol. 74, No. 1190, Voluntary Action supplement, p. ii

Applying to trusts can seem a hit or miss affair and is particularly difficult for newly formed voluntary groups without contacts. It is important to do initial research thoroughly so effort isn't wasted by applying to inappropriate trusts. Local trusts are often best to start off with and information on small local trusts is easier to come by in areas served by a charity information service. Advice on what information to include in the application is given.

133. **Mills, R.**
'Raising money from charitable trusts'
Trust News, Spring 1983, pp. 6–7

This article begins with a section about the basic task of thinking through and formulating the project for which funding is wanted. The following sections deal with identifying which trusts to approach and framing an application. It ends by drawing attention to the importance of follow-up.

134. **Northern Ireland Trusts Group**
Independent Funding for Voluntary Action in Northern Ireland
Northern Ireland Trusts Group, no date, 12pp.

This leaflet was produced to help voluntary groups in Northern Ireland looking for independent sources of funding. It gives information on 16 trusts which give all or a proportion of their grants to groups in Northern Ireland.

135. **Norton, M.**
Raising Money from Trusts
Directory of Social Change, 1981, 118pp.

This is a practical guide to raising money from grant-making trusts. It covers how trusts operate, how to find the right trusts, making the approach and writing an application. It includes contributions from several trust secretaries on how they deal with applications.

136. **Saunders, M.**
Directory of Grant Making Trusts and Organisations for Scotland
Scottish Council for Community and Voluntary Organisations, 2nd edition, 1986, 75pp.

The directory lists over 320 trusts which give grants to voluntary organisations and to individuals in need. Each entry gives the trust's address, telephone number, objects, areas of benefit and the amount of grant normally awarded. There are geographical, subject and name indexes.

137. **Villemur, A.**
Directory of Grant-Making Trusts
Charities Aid Foundation, 9th edition, 1985, 978pp.

The latest edition of this directory contains details of the location, objects, policies and resources of over 2,400 grant-making bodies with a total income of over £482 million.

The directory is in four parts. Part One – a classification of charitable purposes, lists all the principal fields of interest used in recording the allocation of donations by trusts. Part Two lists trusts under the classification categories. Part Three lists the trusts alphabetically and gives details of address, objects, types of grant etc. Part Four contains a geographical index and a subject index. An introductory chapter gives advice on how to approach trusts.

138. **Villemur, A.**
Getting Together with Trusts: A resume of the 1983/84 series of meetings on the theme 'How to approach charities'
Charities Aid Foundation, 1984, 4pp.

This leaflet looks at trusts from a variety of angles using a series of questions to find out what a trust is, what type of project is more likely to succeed with an application, and what type of project trusts look for. There are further sections on beneficiaries, classification and the processing of appeals. The ratio of successful appeals to unsuccessful is examined. Advice is given on how to present an application form and the format it should take.

139. **Waddilove, L. E.**
Private Philanthropy and Public Welfare: The Joseph Rowntree Memorial Trust 1954–1979
George Allen & Unwin, 1983, 237pp.

This is an account of the changes and growth in the constitution and work of the Joseph Rowntree Memorial Trust. The trustees' experience in reconstructing the trust is described. This involved a long debate with public authorities to secure parliamentary approval to the changes in the trustees' powers they found necessary in order to pursue the radical changes in policy they wanted. An account is given of the development of the trust's policy and the innovation made possible by the extension of the powers of the trustees.

140. **Whitaker, B.**
The Foundations: An anatomy of philanthropic societies
Penguin Books, revised edition, 1979, 287pp.

This is a critical analysis of the world's charitable trusts and the people who run them. Between them, these philanthropic funds control enormous sums of money dispensed according to rules they set themselves. The author looks at how the funds operate, their motives, achievements and why they raise suspicion. A chapter giving advice to applicants to the funds on the 'art of grantsmanship' is included.

141. **Younger, C. *et al*. (Editors)**
Trust News
Trust News, three times a year

Trust News describes itself as an 'independent venture' and represents no formal organisation. It includes news and articles on funding from charitable trusts in general as well as on the policies and methods of operation of particular trusts. Its main intended audience is trustees of grant-making trusts, but potential applicants to trusts will also find it of interest.

4.2 Statutory sources of funding

4.2.1 General references

142. **Councils for Voluntary Service – National Association**
Short-Term Money for Voluntary Organisations: A guidance note on the implications of short-term government funding
CVS-NA, 1985, 2pp.
(CVS-NA Circulation; 101, 30 August 1985)

The purpose of this note is to help CVS and their constituent voluntary organisations consider the issues and implications of using government funds which are likely to be of limited duration. Involvement in a funding programme may have considerable effect on the community, participants and the sponsoring organisation. The issues involved are identified and the final decision on whether to use short-term money should involve balancing the advantages and disadvantages.

143. **Ferris, K.**
Better Than a Poke in the Eye . . .': A study of community-based employment initiatives in Lewisham
Voluntary Action Lewisham, Employment Development Unit, 1984, 146pp.

Chapter 2, pages 23–49, of this study is entitled 'Funding for employment and training schemes: where and how'. It: 1. describes the formal and informal criteria and procedure involved in getting resources to set up employment and training initiatives; 2. gives advice on where and how to apply for funding and 3. identifies areas where improvements can be made by funding agencies and in the ways community organisations can help each other.

144. **Heginbotham, C.**
'Money worries'
Social Services Insight, 8–15 March 1986, Vol. 1, No. 10, pp. 22–23

Much voluntary sector funding is insecure. Hassles over small amounts of money and lengthy delays in approval of grants seem to be the major concern of many voluntary sector managers. Delays in processing grants cause wasted time in pursuing grant applications, effective forward planning is undermined and there are serious morale problems when staff contracts can't be renewed. There are some examples of good practice; but how often is seed money wasted because of lack of a long-term guarantee or development periods which are too short? The author believes Government and local authorities must develop clear mechanisms and proper criteria for funding voluntary organisations.

145. **Home Office Voluntary Services Unit**
Monitoring and Evaluation for Grant Givers; Report of a workshop organised jointly by the Charitable Trusts Administrators Group and the Home Office Voluntary Services Unit on 18th January 1984
Home Office Voluntary Services Unit, 1984, 31pp.

Increased pressure on resources raises questions for grant-givers on the best use of resources, about the effectiveness and efficiency of organisations that are funded and about the provision of resources for the purpose of monitoring and evaluation. Grant-makers are paying more attention to accountability, taking a closer interest in what clients do and achieve, and the extent to which their activities are in accord with current policy. How this is done is crucial. It can be seen as a policing task or as part of a development process, enabling organisations to pursue their task more effectively and efficiently. The workshop looks at how monitoring and evaluation can be made useful and creative to both grant-givers and clients.

146. **Jackson, J.**
Threat or Challenge?: Financial management initiatives
Scottish Council for Community and Voluntary Organisations, 1985, 7pp.

Recently, the government has shown an increasing interest in ensuring value for money. We've seen the Rayner scrutinies, the three Es: economy, effectiveness, and efficiency and now the Financial Management Initiative (FMI). Voluntary organisations are being affected since government departments and local authorities will wish to ensure that the organisations they fund meet the new criteria required by FMI. The author explains what FMI is, how the introduction of FMI investigations could affect the voluntary sector, and how its application needs to be modified to take account of the nature of the voluntary sector.

147. **Jones, M.**
Government Grants: A guide for voluntary organisations
Bedford Square Press/NCVO, 3rd edition, 1985, 56pp.

This guide brings together information about grants from central government departments, from quangos, from local authorities and from the European Community. Its intention is to provide groups with guidance about whether they would be eligible for a particular source of grant aid. Each entry gives general information about the types of grant given and the sort of work which can be funded and in some cases gives examples of projects which have received funding. Contact names and addresses are given. Advice on how to apply for a grant is also given.

148. **London Voluntary Service Council, Volunteers Advisory Service**
    Checklist of Funding Sources for Voluntary Work
    LVSC, VAS, 1984, 6pp.

    The aim of this paper is to provide those concerned with organising volunteers or voluntary action projects with a checklist of the main funding resources and funding programmes currently available, brief details on each one, and details of where to go for further information.

149. **National Council for Voluntary Organisations**
    The Management and Effectiveness of Voluntary Organisations
    NCVO, 1984, 20pp.

    Local and central government have increased their funds to voluntary organisations enormously over the last 15 years. Both central and local government have become increasingly concerned to promote 'value for money' and effective accountability in the use of public funds. Because the views of political parties have become more polarised, it is difficult for voluntary organisations to avoid political controversy. Voluntary and statutory agencies need to adjust to these changes. This paper, produced by a review group specifically set up to look at these issues, outlines desirable changes.

    Recommendations are given on the relationship between voluntary organisations and their state funders, on the financial accountability of organisations receiving grants, on the evaluation of an organisation's performance and effectiveness, and on the political activities of charities.

150. **National Council for Voluntary Organisations**
    Relations Between the Voluntary Sector and Government: A code for voluntary organisations
    NCVO, revised edition, 1986, 1pp.

    This code gives guidance to voluntary organisations on achieving a balanced relationship with the government agencies from which they get funding.

151. **Norton, M.**
    Raising Money from Government
    Directory of Social Change, 2nd edition, 1985, 150pp.

    Raising Money from Government looks at sources of government grants under three main headings: getting money from central government; getting money from Quangos; getting money from local government. Apart from details of the the type of grant available including contact addresses, the section on central government funding gives a checklist for organisations looking for central government money. It also has articles on how to approach central government, on the role of the Voluntary Services Unit and on funding from the Urban Programme.

The section on Quangos includes details of grants from, for example, the Commission for Racial Equality, the Equal Opportunities Commission and the Manpower Services Commission, as well as articles on housing projects and associations and financing trips abroad.

The local government section gives details of the legal basis for local authority giving. It also has articles on local authority funding from a grant-seeker's viewpoint, a councillor's viewpoint, and a council officer's viewpoint.

152. **Scott, D. and Wilding, P.**
What Price Voluntary Action?
Manchester Council for Voluntary Service and Manchester University, Department of Social Administration, 1985, 36pp.

This book contains a series of papers presented to a seminar to explore the sponsorship of voluntary bodies and their relation to the state. The longest paper is from Nicholas Hinton, then director of the National Council for Voluntary Organisations, on 'The Role of Government Sponsorship: Encouragement or Interference?' Further papers continue the discussion on statutory funding of voluntary organisations.

4.2.2 Central government and quangos

153. **Abbott, M.**
'Growth in use of volunteers'
Scope, August 1984, No. 75, pp. 6–8

This article talks about the schemes introduced by the government in Northern Ireland over the last few years which offer funding for providing volunteering opportunities. Between 1981–83 the Department of Health and Social Services allocated £300,000 before responsibility was transferred to the Department of Economic Development. DED launched the Community Volunteering Scheme. The way in which two organisations have used funding from the scheme to incorporate volunteers more fully into their work is described.

154. **Berstein, M.**
'Something will turn up'
Community Care, 6 September 1984, No. 528, pp. 25–26

In the context of cuts in service provision, the Government is using short-term DHSS funding initiatives for the voluntary sector to demonstrate it is doing something to promote developmental work in the personal social services.

44

Beyond the short-term, Mike Berstein has little confidence in the maintenance of work initiated by such schemes. One such recent initiative which provides funding for intermediate treatment projects is used to illustrate the drawbacks of such short-term funding initiatives.

155. **Bryant, P.**
Opportunities for Volunteering in Wales: A review of grant applications 1982–1985
Opportunities for Volunteering in Wales, 1985, 43pp.

Since the Opportunities for Volunteering in Wales scheme began in 1982 it has received over 600 applications. The information contained in the applications offered an opportunity to examine the characteristics of organisations applying and their proposed projects. This report describes a study into the distribution and characteristics of the applicants, the level of funding being sought and provided, the types of projects proposed and the use made of available resources.

156. **Cabinet Office (MPO)/Treasury Financial Management Unit**
Policy Work and the FMI
HM Treasury, 1985, Various paginations

This report looks at the implications of the Government's financial management initiative (FMI) for policy analysis and evaluation in government departments concentrating on how departments assess what their programmes of expenditure are actually achieving. This is done through case studies. Case Study Six is 'Home Office – Grants to voluntary organisations administered by the Voluntary Services Unit'. The focus of the case study is on the VSU's grant-giving function and its role in a) monitoring and evaluating organisations receiving or applying for funding and b) monitoring the environment and steering the grant-giving programme towards developing areas (eg race issues) when this is seen as desirable.

157. **Consortium on Opportunities for Volunteering**
DHSS Opportunities for Volunteering Scheme:
Application form for grants
Notes for applicants for grants
Guidelines for applicants
Consortium on Opportunities for Volunteering, updated as necessary.

The notes accompanying the application forms for Opportunities for Volunteering grants describe the scheme's criteria for funding, what grants can be used for and how the grants are administered. The *Guidelines for applicants* give advice on how to complete the application form.

158. **Department of the Environment**
The Urban Programme: Tackling racial disadvantage
Department of the Environment, 1984, 58pp.

This describes 43 Urban Programme funded projects run by black groups and local authorities which are designed to benefit ethnic minorities.

159. **Development Commission**
Annual Reports
Development Commission, annual

The Development Commission is empowered to give financial support to organisations furthering the economic and social development of rural areas in England. Its annual reports give information on grants awarded in the previous year. Voluntary projects benefiting in 1984/85 included an advisory service for the unemployed in Derbyshire, a playbus in Cambridgeshire and 48 projects involving volunteers.

160. **Doyle, M. and Mocroft, I.**
'Opps for Vols – pump-priming a dry well'
Involve, April 1986, No. 50, pp. 10–12

Opportunities for Volunteering began as an experimental one-year funding programme in 1982. Four years later, it is still in operation with a larger budget and now able to fund projects for up to three years. The scheme is moving towards a more important role in the funding of the voluntary sector and its continuation leads the authors to ask questions on three issues: its effectiveness in getting money to the local voluntary sector and its effect on the organisations that use it; the impact it has had on volunteering in terms of numbers, practice and image; its role in relation to the unemployed.

161. **Elliott, S., Lomas, G. and Riddell, A.**
Community Projects Review: A review of voluntary projects receiving Urban Programme funding
Department of the Environment, 1984, 48pp. + appendices

This report sets out the observations, conclusions and recommendations of a review team set up by the Secretary of State for the Environment to examine the support the Urban Programme is giving to voluntary groups. Thirty eight groups in Birmingham, Hammersmith and Fulham were visited. The report concludes the voluntary sector is generally doing a worthwhile job and the funds put into it are well used, but weaknesses were identified. The report recommends improved co-operation between voluntary groups and local government, a more clearly defined approach on the part of central government to the role of the voluntary sector in inner cities and to the assessment of proposals for Urban Programme funding, and a more critical and regular assessment of the effectiveness and achievements of voluntary projects.

162. Fuller, S.
'Focus on Opportunities for Volunteering'
Involve, February 1985, No. 41, pp. 4–5

Sue Fuller uses data from applications to Opportunities for Volunteering in 1983/84 to give an overview of the scheme: the size of grant awarded, the number of staff employed by the projects, the client groups served and the kind of work done by the projects. Common problems are getting the project off the ground once funding is awarded and recruiting volunteers. Six projects funded under the scheme are described.

163. Hodson, P. and Marsh, N.
The Urban Programme Explained (NCVO Information Sheet; No. 27)
NCVO, revised edition, 1986, 7pp.

The Urban Programme is putting more than £70 million into voluntary and community projects in 1985/86. This information sheet outlines what the Urban Programme is, how it works and what voluntary organisations can use it for.

164. Hughes, R. D.
Government Funding and How to Apply: Speech to Oxfordshire CVS,
14 November 1983
(Home Office, Voluntary Services Unit), 1983, 8pp.

Robin Hughes, consultant to the Voluntary Services Unit at the time of giving this speech, talks about the practicalities of approaching the government for funding and provides some principles which will enable anyone looking for funds to assess their position, decide how to make the approach and see it through. Advice on what needs to be done before making contact, how to choose who to approach and the types of funding available is given.

165. Hughes, R. D.
Paper Based on an Address to Birmingham Charitable Trusts Group,
22 March 1983
Home Office, Voluntary Services Unit, 1983, 15pp.

Robin Hughes believes that the changed political and economic environment indicate the need for a fresh approach from grant-makers. In the past, the principal criterion of funders was 'innovation' in an environment where once an initiative got off the ground, there would be other sources of funding to keep it going. This is no longer the case, so innovation as a criterion is no longer applicable.

A recent development has been the increasing role of central government in funding local voluntary organisations, and with a pro-active approach rather than, as in the past, with a reactive approach. Now government grant-makers are defining what they want to pay for and it is up to voluntary organisations to decide if they want to fit in. There is a shift away from a situation where priorities for voluntary action are determined locally to one where they are determined centrally with government setting the priorities.

The author discusses what he sees as the implications of this for other grant-makers in providing independent sources of finance for voluntary action. He suggests independent funders need to increase the capability of voluntary organisations to control their own affairs, to increase the survivability of small and new organisations and to get more of them involved in trading activities as an instrument of community development that brings money with it.

166. **Humble, S.** *et al.*
Opportunities for Volunteering 1982–85: The implementation of the scheme and its performance in meeting the Department's principal aims: A report to the Department of Health and Social Security by the Monitoring Team
The Volunteer Centre and Centre for Research in Social Policy, Loughborough University of Technology, 1985, 106pp.

The purpose of this report is to provide the Department of Health and Social Security with:
a) an overview of the first three years of the Opportunities for Volunteering scheme;
b) information on the implementation of the scheme by the national agents;
c) an appraisal of the scheme's success in recruiting and deploying unemployed volunteers;
d) information on the future funding for projects when their period of funding ends.

167. **Jackson, H.**
'Developing local voluntary action: four experimental small grants schemes'
Home Office Research Bulletin, 1983, No. 16, pp. 51–53

Fund raising is particularly difficult for projects trying to get off the ground. With this in mind, the Home Office Voluntary Services Unit set up a series of local experiments to see what could be achieved by making available resources specifically for launching new projects. The schemes attracted a large number of applicants, but few of the projects were innovatory in the sense of developing new approaches to problems. This may simply suggest expectations were unrealistic, but it also raises the more fundamental issue of the value of the type of short-term funding provided under the scheme.

168. **Kingsley, S.**
'Voluntary action: innovation and experiment as criteria for funding'
Home Office Research Bulletin, 1981, No. 11, pp. 7–9

This article explores an area which seems to be crucial to the way in which voluntary organisations are seen to operate and the way in which many of the programmes initiated by voluntary organisations are funded, that is, the extent to which voluntary organisations produce innovative and experimental programmes, as 'trail-blazers' for statutory services. The author questions the assumption that voluntary organisations are innovatory in comparison with statutory agencies. But following from the notion that voluntary organisations are innovative, funding of a substantial proportion of their programmes has been justified on the basis that they are only for limited experimental periods. Such funding has a major influence on the types of services an organisation attempts to promote and on the development of the organisation itself. Organisations dependent on short-term experimental funding are reactive and insecure and are thus less able to formulate truly innovative approaches to problems. The problems this short-term experimental funding gives rise to and the pressures it places on voluntary organisations are discussed.

169. **Lambert, C. M.**
Departmental Grants etc. 1984: A selection of DoE/DTp awards, funds, grants, initiatives, projects, schemes etc.
Departments of the Environment and Transport Library, 1984, 65pp.

This guide gives details of 57 Department of the Environment and Department of Transport grant schemes, many of which provide funding for voluntary groups. It is the first edition of what was expected to become a regular publication, but up to the time of going to press, there were no plans to produce an updated edition.

170. **Local Development Agencies Development Fund**
Information Pack
LDADF, 1985, Pack of leaflets

From 1986, £1 million a year for three years is being made available through the Voluntary Services Unit at the Home Office to provide funds for the development of existing and new local development agencies. This pack explains the aims of the fund, the criteria and conditions of receiving a grant from the fund and gives details of how to apply.

171. **Manpower Services Commission**
The Community Programme
MSC, 1985, 12pp.

This booklet explains the aims of the Community Programme, what is involved in being a sponsor and how to apply.

172. **Manpower Services Commission**
Community Programme News
Manpower Services Commission, Irregular (Approximately 4–5 issues a year)

This newsletter reports on the Community Programme and Voluntary Projects Programme.

173. **Manpower Services Commission**
Voluntary Projects Programme
MSC, (no date), 11pp.

The Voluntary Projects Programme aims to provide a variety of opportunities for unemployed people to take up on a voluntary basis. This leaflet explains what type of projects are funded under the scheme.

174. **National Council for Voluntary Organisations**
Government Initiatives on Volunteering, Volunteering for the Unemployed, Youth Training (NCVO Information Sheet; No. 25)
NCVO, revised edition, 1986, 8pp.

This information sheet outlines four government schemes in which voluntary organisations may participate: the Youth Training Scheme, the Community Programme, the Voluntary Projects Programme and Opportunities for Volunteering. It is intended to clarify the differences and overlap between them.

175. **National Council for Voluntary Organisations**
Voluntary Projects Programme
NCVO Employment Unit, 1984, 4pp.

This booklet explains what type of projects are funded under the Voluntary Projects Programme and gives contacts for voluntary organisations needing further advice.

176. **National Council for Voluntary Organisations Community Schemes Unit**
Reporter
National Council for Voluntary Organisations Community Schemes Unit, Bi-monthly

This newsletter provides news and information on the Youth Training Scheme to voluntary sector YTS projects.

177. National Council for Voluntary Organisations Urban Unit
Inter-City Network
National Council for Voluntary Organisations Urban Unit, 10 issues a year

Inter-City Network reports on matters of interest to urban voluntary organisations, including news of developments in the Urban Programme.

178. Scottish Community Education Council
Urban Aid Explained
Scottish Community Education Council, revised edition, 1985, 37pp.

This pamphlet explains the Urban Programme for voluntary groups in Scotland – what types of project urban aid funds and how to apply.

179. Scottish Council for Community and Voluntary Organisations
A Guide to Government Grants for Voluntary Organisations in Scotland
SCCVO, 1982, 27pp.

This directory gives information on grants available from central government departments and quangos to voluntary groups in Scotland. Each entry includes information about the nature of the grants, the purposes for which they are given and the means of application.

180. Simmonds, D.
The Community Programme Expansion and Voluntary Projects Programme Development: An NCVO briefing
(Special Employment Measures Update, No. 1, Supplementary Special Issue)
National Council for Voluntary Organisations Employment Unit, 1985, 11pp.

This briefing outlines the measures announced in the 1985 budget for the development of the Community Programme and Voluntary Projects Programme. The details of the programmes at the time the briefing was issued were still being worked on and were subject to change. The briefing raises questions about the direction of CP and VPP and how these affect voluntary organisations.

181. Simmonds, D. and Richards, A. (Editors)
Special Employment Measures Update
National Council for Voluntary Organisations Employment Unit, No. 1, Sept. 1985

This information bulletin is aimed at voluntary sector sponsors of Manpower Services Commission funded Special Employment Measures (SEMs). It aims to inform sponsors of changes in the operation of SEMs and keep voluntary organisations abreast of policy discussions on them. Occasional factsheets on particular issues are published with the bulletin.

182. Stubbings, P.
The Smile on the Face of the Tiger
The Volunteer Centre Employment Unit, 1984, 8pp.

In 1981 the Prime Minister announced measures to ease unemployment, including two to give unemployed people the opportunity to do voluntary work. The voluntary sector was not consulted and in implementing both the Voluntary Projects Programme and Opportunities for Volunteering, the Government ran up against a mismatch of its goals and those of the voluntary sector. The programmes have brought difficulties as well as benefits for their users. Some of the main criticisms are: funding is normally for 12 months or less, so a lot of effort is put into getting further funding; staff and volunteers work in an atmosphere of insecurity and anxiety; the criteria for selection of projects are often inappropriate; heavy demands are made on a sponsoring organisation's core structure and resources by the need to manage new money, staff, volunteers and activities; inadequate support and information is received from grant-givers. The voluntary sector needs to look more closely at such funding when it is offered and decide if it is appropriate for what they want to do instead of accepting it without question.

183. Unell, J.
Opportunity Costs: Government funding and volunteering by unemployed young people
National Youth Bureau, 1984, 24pp.

This is an investigation into two government funding schemes to help unemployed people to volunteer – Opportunities for Volunteering and the Voluntary Projects Programme. It looks at the wider policy issues arising from the impact of government initiatives upon patterns of community involvement among young people and also at ways in which local agencies have taken up the new funding opportunities.

The management of one-off packages of funding from central government is an issue of increasing concern to voluntary organisations. Such funding is usually short-term and is intended to encourage innovation around specific issues or areas of provision rather than support 'core' activities of an organisation. Long-term changes in the pattern and direction of an agency's work are therefore being stimulated within the context of short-term financial support. So the implications of participtation in such a funding programme need careful consideration. From the study of the Opportunities for Volunteering and VPP schemes, lessons are drawn about involvement in short-term funding programmes.

184. Wales Council for Voluntary Action
Guide to Grant Aid for Voluntary Organisations in Wales: No. 1. Welsh Office grants
WCVA, 1984, 9pp.

This guide provides basic information about the kinds of grants the Welsh Office is able to make to voluntary organisations in Wales. It covers grants in the fields of health and personal social services, youth, education, gypsies, environment, housing, and transport.

185. **Wales Council for Voluntary Action**
Urban Aid in Wales: A guide for voluntary groups
(Information Sheet; No. 7)
WCVA 1986, 4pp.

This information sheet aims to help voluntary organisations in Wales apply for urban aid funds. It explains the aim of the programme, the conditions under which grant aid is given, and how to go about applying.

186. **Westland, P.**
'No sense of direction'
Community Care, 17 November 1983, No. 488, pp. 15–17

There has been a spate of announcements of new Department of Health and Social Security initiatives in the voluntary sector usually accompanied by much publicity. The schemes tend to be short-term and no indication is given of where funding will come from for projects financed under a particular scheme once it is finished. The author believes that as social policy measures, these initiatives are marginal and probably short-lived. Their value is over-emphasised. They have a desperate and sometimes weary air about them and are a poor substitute for a sense of direction.

187. **Willis, E.**
Quickstep and Side Kick: The dance of a twelve month funded worker
The Volunteer Centre, Employment Unit, 1984, 4pp.

Many project workers in voluntary organisations must be familiar with the strains imposed by working on a short-term contract unsure if funding will be renewed. The author describes the effects of such short-term funding on her attitude to work and way of working.

188. **Wright, P. (Editor)**
'Voluntary organisations and the MSC: managing the Community Programme'
MDU Bulletin, December 1985, No. 6, 24pp.

This issue of the *MDU Bulletin* addresses itself to the management problems facing voluntary organisations which receive government funding. In particular, does the voluntary sector's increasing participation in government funded programmes threaten its independence?

The articles are written by people involved with voluntary sector projects funded mainly by the Community Programme and look at the relationship between the projects and their funding agency, the Manpower Services Commission.

4.2.3 Local government

189. **Association of County Councils, National Council for Voluntary Organisations and Association of Metropolitan Authorities**
Working Together: Partnerships in local social service
Bedford Square Press/NCVO, 1981, 53pp.

The working party which compiled this report aimed to offer guidance on principles and procedures which will sustain the relationships between local authority social service departments and local voluntary organisations and community groups. It considers local authority grant-aid procedures, the factors which influence the allocation of grants, and what obligations are placed on a voluntary organisation which receives local authority funding. In short, it is a record of good practice which is intended to be helpful to voluntary organisations in their dealings with their local authority funders and vice versa.

190. **Broady, M.**
The Statutory Authority and Voluntary Social Welfare: A review of Thamesdown Borough Council's policy on grant-aiding voluntary organisations
Maurice Broady (University College Swansea), 1983, 116pp.

This is a report commissioned by the Planning Committee of Thamesdown Borough Council to review the Council's policy on grants to voluntary organisations and the management of community centres by community groups grant-aided by the Committee.

The author looked at the Council's support for the voluntary sector and its criteria for grant aid. He also considered the accountability of organisations receiving aid and if the Council is getting value for the money it allocates to voluntary organisations. He concludes that Thamesdown Borough Council is getting value for money and recommends increasing its financial support of voluntary organisations.

191. **Crawford, C. and Moore, V.**
'The Free Two Pence': Section 137 of the Local Government Act 1972 and Section 83 of the Local Government (Scotland) Act 1973
The Chartered Institute of Public Finance and Accountancy, 1983, 218pp.

S.137 and S.83 allow local authorities to spend, subject to a maximum of a 2p rate for any one authority in any one year, in the interests of all or part of that authority and all or some of its inhabitants on any matters which are not otherwise provided for by any other enactment.

This study examines these provisions by explaining their history and background, the operation of the powers, the problems surrounding their use, and by discussing the options open in any change or reform. The purpose of the study was to fill a gap since no information was available on the ways in which these powers are used or the extent of their use. Questionnaires sent to all principal authorities in England, Wales and Scotland received a 94.6% response rate. The results of the survey showed that only 53.4% of authorities had used the power at any time in the period from re-organisation to the end of the financial year 1981/82. The expenditure in 1981/82 expressed as a percentage of the sum available to these authorities using the power was 11%. In 1982/83 this figure rose to 23.9%. The survey shows that S.137 and S.83 are used for a wide variety of purposes including funding voluntary organisations. Over the whole country in the financial year 1981/82 £6,475,755 was donated to charities under these provisions.

192. **Department of the Environment, Scottish Office and Welsh Office**
Submission to the Committee of Inquiry into the Conduct of Local Authority Business: The use of local authorities' discretionary spending powers
Department of the Environment, 1985, 22pp.

This joint submission to the Widdicombe Inquiry considers the way in which local authorities use the discretionary powers given to them under S.137 of the Local Government Act 1972 and S.83 of the Local Government (Scotland) Act 1973. The Departments are concerned that public funds are being used to finance organisations of a 'partisan and controversial nature' and 'to set up and support organisations only partially subject to adequate requirements for public accountability and statutory control'. It is the Departments' view that if general discretionary powers are to be retained they must be accompanied by measures to ensure effective accountability and to prevent politically interested exploitation.

193. **Forsyth, M. B.**
Politics on the Rates: How the left are using public money to finance their activities
Conservative Political Centre, 1984, 24pp.

Mr. Forsyth, a Conservative MP, believes local authority money is misused by giving grants to left-wing, politically active organisations. Most of this funding is authorised using Section 137 of the Local Government Act 1972. The author believes reform is needed to prevent what he sees as abuse by local authorities of the powers given to them under Section 137.

194. **Gorman, T. et al.**
Qualgos Just Grow: Political bodies in voluntary clothing
Centre for Policy Studies, 1985, 47pp.

The authors of this report believe that local authority funding to voluntary organisations often goes to left-wing politically-motivated organisations which are not voluntary in the sense in which most people understand this term. They believe this is a misuse of ratepayers' money. Local government funding of QUALGOS (Quasi-Autonomous Local Government Organisations), particularly through Section 137 of the Local Government Act 1972, is looked at through case studies. Recommendations to councils on how they should evaluate requests for grants are made along with suggestions for increasing the accountability of voluntary organisations and tightening up the regulations which govern local authority funding of voluntary organisations. *(See also ref. No. 205)*

195. **Grey, A. and Johnson, C.**
London Boroughs Grants Scheme: Grants to voluntary organisations in London: the new scheme: final report
HAY-MSL Management Consultants Group Ltd, 1985, 39pp.

This report outlines how the London Boroughs Grants Scheme will work when implemented. Eligibility criteria and decision making procedures are covered. Consideration is given to the role of the new unit and its organisational structure, including staffing and computing facilities.

196. **Hencke, D.**
'Livingstone's lifeline'
Voluntary Action, Autumn 1983, No. 16, pp. 6–7

In 1983/84 the Greater London Council gave £34 million in grants to voluntary organisations. GLC funding of voluntary organisations increased dramatically within the previous two years. David Hencke looks at the impact of the GLC's grants policy on London's voluntary sector and speculates that abolition of the GLC could do much to damage London voluntary organisations, including national organisations based in London.

197. **Leat, D.**
'Making sense of grant aid'
Charity Statistics, 1984/85, pp. 45–49

A study undertaken by the Policy Studies Institute attempted to examine the effects on voluntary organisations of receiving statutory grant aid. The researchers encountered difficulty in finding out exactly how much grant aid is given and also in making meaningful comparisons between authorities because of the different methods used by authorities in recording aid to voluntary organisations. The study also looked at 'hidden' aid in the form of low rent or rent-free premises, the provision of photocopying and printing facilities etc. It was found that this type of help can amount to a considerable proportion of the total aid given by local authorities to the voluntary sector.

Another aspect of the study concentrated on the policy and practices on grant aid. The most common explanation of the level of grant aid in any particular authority is tradition and precedent; the voluntary sector gets what it does today because that is more or less what it got last year.

198. Leat, D., Tester, S., and Unell, J.
A Price Worth Paying?: A study of the effects of government grant aid to voluntary organisations
Policy Studies Institute, 1986, 201pp.

This study looks at the effect of local government grant aid to voluntary organisations. It focuses on four key questions. What effect does statutory grant aid have on the number of paid staff employed? Does it affect the level of volunteer involvement? How does it change the amount of funding obtained from other sources? And does it undermine the independence of organisations getting grants?

The evidence from the study suggests that statutory grant aid, far from ' undermining voluntarism, actually encourages it and creates the conditions for development.

199. London Voluntary News
'The Richmond scheme'
London Voluntary News, June/July 1985, No. 205, pp. 1–2

This article looks at the recently published report on the London Boroughs Grant Scheme, which sets out arrangements for funding of voluntary organisations in London after the abolition of the Greater London Council. Criteria for receiving grant aid, the decision making process and responsibilities of the grant unit are outlined. The report was generally well received at a council meeting of the London Voluntary Service Council but points for anxiety remained. A run down of the achievements and disappointments of the voluntary sector over the 21 months since the abolition proposals appeared is given. Arrangements for transitional funding are described.

200. London Voluntary Service Council
Funding for Voluntary Organisations after the GLC
LVSC, 1985, 2pp.

This briefing summarises the proposals for the continuing of grant aid to voluntary and community groups after the abolition of the Greater London Council.

201. London Voluntary Service Council
Funding London's Voluntary Sector
LVSC, 1984, 4pp.

This briefing gives an overview of the pattern of funding of London's voluntary sector at a time when the forthcoming abolition of the GLC was causing much uncertainty about future funding. Figures are given for the total amount given by the four principal statutory sources of funding: the GLC, London boroughs, the Urban Programme and the Joint boroughs scheme. Examples of particular projects with a breakdown of where each of them gets their funding are also given.

202. Major, E. and Ashworth, M.
'Local authority support of charitable bodies'
Charity Statistics, 1984/85, pp. 11–44

This article presents information collected from all tiers of local authority (except parish councils) in England, Wales and Scotland on fees and grants paid by local authorities to voluntary bodies in 1983/84. The results of the survey are summarised and figures for each individual authority responding to the survey are also given.

203. Morgan, M.
A Review of Local Authority Aid to Voluntary Organisations in the London Borough of Croydon
Croydon Guild of Voluntary Organisations, 1984, 41pp.

The main finding of this research report shows that the departmental structure of local government is not conducive to a co-ordinated approach to providing help to voluntary organisations. The resulting diversity of grant aid services and procedures is confusing for voluntary organisations. This confusion is made worse by the lack of information about the process and the absence of consultative machinery between the council and the voluntary sector.

The review recommended setting up a joint consultative committee, the designation of a member of council staff to act as a central information and referral point, publication of an explanatory booklet, and making council agendas and minutes publicly available.

204. National Council for Voluntary Organisations
Voluntary Organisations and Local Government: Submission to the Committee of Inquiry into the Conduct of Local Authority Business
NCVO, 1985, 31pp.

NCVO's evidence to the Widdicombe Inquiry discusses the contribution voluntary organisations make to the local democratic process. Local authority funding of voluntary organisations through the discretionary powers given to local authorities under Section 137 of the Local Government Act 1972 are discussed. Local authorities use of this power has been criticised. NCVO makes suggestions for increasing accountability and encouraging good practice in the future.

205. National Council for Voluntary Organisations
The Voluntary Sector: A response to the Centre for Policy Studies publication 'Qualgos just grow' subtitled 'Political bodies in voluntary clothing'
NCVO, 1985, 31pp.

The authors of *Qualgos Just Grow (see ref. No. 194)* are criticised for misunderstanding the voluntary sector and the nature of the partnership between local authorities and the voluntary sector. By explaining its nature and role, this response to *Qualgos Just Grow* aims to promote better understanding of the voluntary sector. The recommendations on the funding of the voluntary organisations by local authorities made in *Qualgos Just Grow* are commented upon. Suggestions for improvements and consolidation of the ground rules governing the funding and operation of voluntary organisations are made.

206. **Raine, J. W. and Webster, B.**
Strategy, Choice and Support: A review of grant-aid to voluntary and community organisations from the London Borough of Camden
University of Birmingham, Institute of Local Government Studies, 1984, 101pp.

Camden Council commissioned this review of its policies and practices on grant aid. The review looked at the current distribution of grants, gaps and duplication in provision, how improvements in the distribution could be made, the implications of any recommended changes and how to improve the monitoring and evaluation of grant-aided projects.

The report makes recommendations to the Council on its policy and strategy on grant aid, the process and pattern of funding, and on the support it provides to the voluntary sector in Camden.

207. **Stubbings, P.**
'How to help volunteer groups without money'
County Councils Gazette, July 1981, Vol. 74, No. 4, pp. 107–109

The author suggests how local authorities can help voluntary organisations other than by giving direct financial aid by, for example, providing accommodation for meetings or for housing a project, giving access to equipment and to staff with particular expertise.

208. **Woollett, S.**
Rural Funds: Aid for local initiatives (Rural Briefing; No. 10)
National Council for Voluntary Organisations Rural Department, 1981, 5pp.

This briefing paper discusses the benefits of local authorities establishing funds to provide grants to local community projects in rural areas. It gives examples of how several schemes already introduced by local authorities operate.

4.3 European Economic Community

209. Commission of the European Communities, London Office
Finance from Europe: A guide to grants and loans from the European Community
Commission of the European Communities London Office, 1983, 21pp. + 6pp. supplement, 1985.

Finance from Europe includes sections on employment and training grants, regional grants, loans for economic development, assistance for developing countries and aid for research and development. Each section gives details of the type of scheme for which assistance is given, the type of organisations eligible, the value of grants given and how to apply.

210. **Davison, A.**
Grants from Europe: How to get money and influence policy
Bedford Square Press/NCVO in association with ERICA (European Research into Consumer Affairs), 3rd edition, 1986, 86pp.

This book explains how the European Economic Community works, what decisions it makes and how to influence policy. It gives information on the funds available, how to apply to them, and key contacts in Brussels and the UK. There are chapters covering funding for: unemployment, poverty, women, ethnic minorities, disabled people, education and culture, the third world, environment and energy and consumer interests.

211. **Dawson, E. and Norton, M.**
Money and Influence in Europe: A guide for voluntary organisations
Directory of Social Change and Voluntary Movement Group, 1983, 149pp.

The first part of this handbook looks at how voluntary organisations can get money from the EEC, in particular from the European Social Fund and Anti-Poverty Programme. The second part considers how to influence policy. Several case studies are given.

212. **Department of Employment**
European Social Fund: Note by the Department of Employment
Department of Employment, annual

Each year, after the European Social Fund publishes details of priorities for funding for the coming year, the Department of Employment issues guidance on how to apply. Since the Department of Employment is the channel for all UK applications, this guidance note is essential for any organisation considering applying to the Fund. It includes information on what sort of schemes qualify for support, how to apply, how much to apply for and current priorities for funding.

213. **Seary, B.**
The European Social Fund: Information for voluntary organisations
National Council for Voluntary Organisations, 1986, 2pp.

The European Social Fund allocated £10 million for voluntary employment projects in 1986. This paper gives brief information for organisations considering applying to the Fund, including details of the sorts of projects currently receiving priority.
The paper is regularly updated.

214. **Wales Council for Voluntary Action**
The European Social Fund (Information Sheet; No. 8)
WCVA, 1985, 6pp.

The European Social Fund provides funding for vocational training and job creation projects. This information sheet explains what support the fund gives and what projects may be eligible for funding. Information is given on the areas which the fund is giving priority to in 1986.

4.4 How to apply for a grant

215. **Chisholm, S.**
'Raising money costs money'
Youth in Society, November 1983, No. 84, pp. 24–25

South Riding Youth Action is a small voluntary organisation with two full-time workers. Although the job description of the organiser explicitly stated that fund raising was not part of the job, no-one else had the time or knowledge to do it effectively. The appeal for money was successful and taught the organiser a few general principles to follow when applying for grants. It is best to apply for specific amounts for specific projects; personal contact with donors is important; high quality applications are essential; good timing and choosing appropriate funders to apply to are also important.

216. **Feek, W.**
Can You Credit It?: Grant-givers' views on funding applications
National Youth Bureau, 1982, 20pp.

This book aims to give help with an aspect of funding agencies not always investigated by applicants – their procedures and thinking for handling applications. How do they view applicants? What information is most important to them? What elements in applications make a good or bad impression, and what contact with the applicant do they like? The views of two members of staff working for funding agencies – a trust and a local authority youth service – are given in interview form.

217. **Feek, W.**
Hitting the Right Notes: Information on applying for funds
National Youth Bureau, 1982, 22pp.

The theory and practice of applying for funds are dealt with in two sections. The theory section outlines a possible format for applying for funds, how best to present your case. The practice is looked at through an interview with members of Nottingham Young Volunteers about their experience of applying for grants.

218. **National Council for Voluntary Organisations Information Department**
How to Apply for a Grant (NCVO Information Sheet; No. 29)
NCVO, 1984, 4pp.

This information sheet explains how to research appropriate sources of funding and how to complete an effective application. An application must be concise, informative and well presented. A list of some guides to raising funds is included.

5 Raising Funds for Particular Causes

5.1 Arts

219. **Arthur Andersen & Co.**
Business Sponsorship of the Arts: A tax guide
Association for Business Sponsorship of the Arts, 1985, 40pp.

Business sponsorship of the arts has grown dramatically in recent years. It is estimated that the total for 1986 will be £20 million. The need to obtain adequate tax relief for this sponsorship is important to the businesses involved. The purpose of this guide is to clarify the tax position of businesses in relation to arts sponsorship. It is also intended to highlight the problems businesses face and to steer them through the current tax system which is often inconsistent.

220. **Barratt, P. C., Fates, S. L. and Meek, K. J. N.**
Corporate Donations and Sponsorship as Sources of Income for the Arts
Charities Aid Foundation, 1980

This report analyses sources of income for the arts in Great Britain. It also gives the results of a questionnaire on charitable donations and sponsorship of the arts sent to over 100 large companies.
A summary of this report appears in *Charity Statistics 1979/80*, pp. 48–58.

221. **Crine, S. *et al*.**
'Funding arts'. Part One
Charity, May 1985, Vol. 2, No. 7, pp. 8–10, 12–15
and
'Funding arts'. Part Two
Charity, June 1985, Vol. 2, No. 8, pp. 13–14

This series of articles starts with a brief review of arts funding in Europe. The other articles in the collection are on: the recently formed National Campaign for the Arts; the Granada Foundation – a charitable trust supporting the arts in North West England; the work of CRYPT (Creative Young People Together) which offers disabled young people residential arts workshops; the National Art Collections Fund; the National Association of Arts Centres; the funding of musicians; and an assessment by the director of the Channel Theatre Company of what new sources of funding may be available to counter impending reductions in grants.

222. **Kelly, O.**
Community, Art and the State: Storming the citadels
Comedia Publishing Group, 1984, 143pp.

Owen Kelly believes the development of community arts in this country has been guided by the types of funding it has received. He recounts a history of community arts to show how the policies of funding agencies have influenced the development of the movement. He establishes the outline of a different strategy, including a look at possible alternative funding sources.

223. **Mullin, R.**
AIM: A report on the Arts Initiative and Money Project 1980–1983
Calouste Gulbenkian Foundation, 1984, 84pp.

The Arts Initiative and Money (AIM) project aimed to help artists and small artistic ventures to make better use of their existing financial and management resources, to exploit their opportunities more effectively, and to understand better the various sources from which help might be drawn. The project worked in two ways. Firstly, it assessed grant applications and passed its recommendations to the Gulbenkian Foundation. Secondly, it initiated projects and research. Twenty five grant recipients and their projects are described.

5.2 Overseas aid and disaster appeals

224. **Attorney General**
Disaster Appeals
Attorney General, 1984, 5pp.

Setting up a public appeal following a disaster is usually done within a very short time. In these circumstances, questions sometimes arise over the status of appeals after they have been set up, as was the case with the Penlee Lifeboat appeal. The Attorney General prepared these guidelines to help those faced with the responsibility of making disaster appeals in the future.

225. **Moorhead, C.**
'Geldof and the givers'
New Society, 18 October 1985, Vol. 74, No. 1190, pp. 99–101

Band Aid Trust, initiated by Bob Geldof after seeing television reports of famine in Ethiopia, made £8 million from its first venture, a Christmas pop record. Band Aid quickly and effectively organised shipping and emergency flights, but left the aid charities working in Africa to decide among themselves where the need was greatest and apply to Band Aid in London for what they wanted.

The next project, Live Aid, two concerts broadcast in 160 countries, brought the Trust another £50 million. Aid experts and charities are being consulted about how the money should be allocated.

The venture has tapped new donors – the young, and the scale of their response surprised even Band Aid organisers. No one can say if the phenomenon will endure, but Band Aid is determined to keep the momentum going.

226. **New Internationalist**
'Voluntary aid'
New Internationalist, **June 1985, No. 148, pp. 7–26**

This issue of *New Internationalist* has a series of articles on charity and the Third World. 'Can you help' looks at the work of the aid charities. 'Accounting for aid' is a survey of the income of voluntary agencies working for the Third World. 'One child at a time' looks at a scheme whereby someone in the West sponsors a child in the Third World. 'A guide to giving' advises on choosing an aid organisation to donate your money to. 'Giving reasons' discusses motivations for giving.

227. **Phillips, A.**
'Disaster: we are not ready yet: the lessons of Penlee that we will not learn'
Charity, **December 1984, Vol. 2, No. 2, pp. 19**

The Penlee disaster exemplified the problems caused when there is an immediate public response to a disaster since there is no existing recognised focal point which can cope with the instant outpouring of public sympathy and funds. The form in which an appeal is set up can easily be found later to run into tax and/or charity law problems. Penlee stimulated one modest initiative. A few months later the Attorney General issued guidelines to assist those caught up in disaster appeals. It is proposed that what is really needed is a National Disaster Fund Organisation to collect and dispose of funds collected for a particular disaster.

228. **Pouncey, P.**
'Ethiopia: media rules, OK?'
Media Project News, **January 1985, pp. 4–6**

TV pictures have the power to motivate public response, and the combined overseas aid charities have raised over £30 million in special joint appeals since 1964. Strong news coverage coincidental with the appeal adds to the success, as with the latest Famine in Africa appeal with a news reporter in Ethiopia. After the appeal had closed, more TV reports brought overwhelming public response. Success raises problems. Too much media coverage brings sensationalism and gives the charities the added burden of answering public and media enquiries. A further problem is to attract media attention to less dramatic need.

5.3 Environmental projects

229. **Countryside Commission**
Conservation Grants for Local Authorities, Public Bodies and Voluntary Organisations
Countryside Commission, 1984, 16pp.

The Countryside Commission provides grant aid for a variety of activities which promote conservation and recreation in the countryside, including recreation footpaths, countryside management projects and voluntary management agreements. This booklet describes the range of grants available to enable voluntary organisations among others to undertake projects which will conserve or enhance the appearance of the countryside.

230. **Kallaway (Sponsorship, Consultancy and Management) Limited**
Conservation and Business Sponsorship
Nature Conservancy Council, 1983, 10pp.

This booklet, sponsored by the Department of the Environment, encourages companies to sponsor organisations working in the field of conservation. Examples of successful sponsorships are given and the advantages to companies pointed out.

231. **Shell Better Britain Campaign**
Shell Better Britain Campaign Information Pack
Shell Better Britain Campaign, Nature Conservancy Council, 1986, folder of leaflets

The Shell Better Britain Campaign supports community initiatives in environmental conservation and improvement. The pack explains what type of projects are eligible for grants and gives advice on setting up and running a project.

232. **Wates, N.**
'Community catalysts'
RIBA Journal, October 1984, Vol. 91, No. 10, pp. 59–62, 65–66.

The Royal Institute of British Architects Community Projects Fund is funded by an annual grant from the Department of the Environment Urban Initiatives Fund (Special Grants Programme) which is matched by RIBA, mainly in staff resources. RIBA uses the money to make small grants to voluntary organisations normally unable to afford professional advice so that they can employ architects to undertake feasibility studies for building and other environmental projects. If the projects obtain capital funding, the money is returned to RIBA and recycled. The 66 projects funded in the first two years of the scheme are very diverse. Details of several projects are given.

233. **White, P.**
'Foundations of optimism for fringes'
Planning, 23 November 1984, No. 596, pp. 8–9

A new environmental body, the Groundwork Foundation, is being launched to support existing Groundwork Trusts and to encourage new ones. These trusts aim to help transform waste urban fringe areas into real countryside. The Foundation will act as a national fund-raiser and distribute part of the income it raises as grants to the various trusts. Initial funding will be given by the Department of the Environment but its main task will be to attract support from business and its importance will come from its attempt to get public and private sectors in partnership in the conservation field.

5.4 Ethnic minorities

234. Baker, W. V.
The Arts of Ethnic Minorities: Status and funding: a research report
Commission for Racial Equality, 1985, 62pp.

An earlier report *The Arts Britain Ignores* demonstrated that ethnic minority arts had largely been ignored by institutions set up to assist and encourage arts in this country. This publication reports on information gathered in interviews with members of ethnic minority arts groups and representatives of funding agencies. A look at government funding in this area shows a confusing picture, with a large number of agencies offering grants but with unclear relationships and little co-ordination between them. There seem to be no clear policies, and despite published statements of commitment, the end result is still one of neglect. In 1980–81, less than 1 per cent of the Arts Council and Regional Arts Associations funding was given to ethnic minority projects. Suggestions are made for improvements in the present system of funding which will help create equality of opportunity for ethnic minority arts projects.

235. Edgington, J. *et al.*
Voluntary Action, Summer 1981, No. 7

This issue of *Voluntary Action* includes several articles on the funding of black self-help groups.
J. Edgington 'Is there a funding blackout?' (Editorial), p. 1
J. Edgington 'Blacks and unemployment programmes', p. 3
L. Mackie 'Are blacks getting the cash?', pp. 6–7
A. Wilson 'Making grants to black groups', pp. 8–9
D. Stockford 'Projects in practice', pp. 10–11

236. Hines, V. (Chairman)
Funding of Black Groups in the UK: The Department of the Environment Informal Working Group on Inner Cities Problems: a response from the black communities
National Federation of Self-Help Organisations, 1983, 15pp.

In 1983 the Department of Environment convened several informal consultative meetings to look at particular aspects. This is the report of the group which looked at inner city problems. Out of these meetings, four informal groups were set up to look at particular aspects. This is the report of the group which looked at the funding of black organisations, arrived at after consultation with appropriate groups including black voluntary organisations and community leaders. The report details the financial and resource needs of black groups; it recommends what response is needed from central government, businesses and trusts to meet these needs, and suggests priorities for the funding of black groups.

237. Leech, K.
The CRRU Projects Fund and its Importance
The British Council of Churches, Race, Pluralism and Community Group, 1982, 8pp.

The CRRU Projects Fund supports groups who are working for racial justice in Britain. This publication describes the criteria for funding and the type of projects which are given grants.

238. The National Federation of Self-Help Organisations
Financing Black-Managed Groups for Community Development: Agreed resolutions (at the) 7th National Convention, Northampton, September 1985
NFSHO, 1985, 8pp.

NFSHO is the main co-ordinating body for self-help organisations, particularly those managed by members of African, West Indian and Asian descent. Resolutions agreed at its seventh convention concerned the development of black businesses and co-operatives, the use of Section 11 of the Local Government Act 1966 for financing black voluntary organisations, funding for black groups from the European Social Fund and on the National Self-Help Fund which was established to provide funding for black-managed organisations.

239. Norton, M. and Blume, H.
Fundraising: A handbook for minority groups
Commission for Racial Equality, 1979, 79pp.
(A new edition is in preparation by the Commission for Racial Equality in conjunction with the Directory for Social Change.)

This handbook examines the sources of funds available to minority groups – central and local government, the Commission for Racial Equality, Urban Aid, the Manpower Services Commission, the Arts Council, trusts, companies and international sources. The authors give some information for particular types of project, such as education, arts and employment projects. Advice on how to apply for a grant is also given.

240. Stares, R.
Insights into Black Self-Help: The Commission for Racial Equality's Self-Help Programme: a review of the activities and performance of ten grant recipients
Commission for Racial Equality, 1984, 45pp.

The Commission for Racial Equality's Self-Help Fund was established in 1974 to provide support to existing black self-help groups and encourage the creation of new ones. This study looks at ten long-established recipients of funding under the scheme. Projects were funded for up to five years and were then expected to become either financially self-supporting or obtain alternative funding. This study was the first independent assessment of the scheme to examine its overall performance and impact.

241. **Stewart, M. and Whitting, G.**
Ethnic Minorities and the Urban Programme
University of Bristol, School for Advanced Urban Studies, 1983, 73pp.

This study, commissioned by the Department of the Environment, looks at assistance to black voluntary groups through the Urban Programme. It assesses the factors which inhibit or encourage the development and funding of projects by or for ethnic minority groups.

5.5 Health and social services

242. **Association of Medical Research Charities**
Handbook of the Association of Medical Research Charities
Association of Medical Research Charities, annual

The foreword to the 1985/86 edition of this handbook states that it seems the only growing contribution to medical research in real terms is that provided by the voluntary sector. The 35 member organisations of the Association of Medical Research Charities had an income of £150 million in 1984 of which almost £90 million was given to medical research. This handbook helps applicants for funds by providing information on each of the Association's members. The aims, activities, financial information and type of award is given for each organisation.

243. **Department of Health and Social Security**
Health Services Development: Care in the community and joint finance
(Circular HC(83)6; LAC(83)5)
Department of Health and Social Security, 1983, 19pp.

Explanatory Notes on Care in the Community
Department of Health and Social Security, 1983, 12pp.

Health Services Development: Collaboration between the NHS, local government and voluntary organisations; Voluntary organisation representation on joint consultative committees, and extension of the joint finance arrangements **(Circular HC(84)9; LAC(84)8)**
Department of Health and Social Security, 1984, (15)pp.

The 1983 circular gives guidance on joint finance arrangements including the circumstances under which voluntary organisations can be given funding. *Explanatory Notes on Care in the Community* was issued at the same time as the circular specifically to help voluntary organisations who wanted to become involved in the care in the community initiative. The 1984 circular gives guidance on the extension of joint finance arrangements and updates the information on conditions governing joint finance payments by health authorities to local authorities and voluntary organisations.

244. **Heginbotham, C.**
Webs and Mazes: Approaches to care in the community
Centre on Environment for the Handicapped, 1984, 47pp.

The intention of this publication is to encourage collaborative approaches to providing care in the community for mentally ill, mentally handicapped, elderly and disabled people by alerting anyone involved to the range of financial mechanisms and the scope for joint agency working. The mechanisms for funding community care schemes are complex and money can come from many sources. The sources described include joint finance and funding under the 'Care in the Community' circular; housing association funding and health service capital for housing and accommodation; funding from the Manpower Services Commission for day care and employment; Urban Aid; Opportunities for Volunteering and the use of welfare benefits.

245. **Hickling, R.**
'Medical research: too much time is spent seeking finance'
Charity, January 1984, Vol. 1, No. 3, pp. 8–10

Roger Hickling, appeal Secretary of the Royal College of Surgeons of England since 1979 and a campaign director for a firm of fund-raising consultants since 1969, describes the different sources, statutory and voluntary, of medical research funding – the Medical Research Council, the 34 major medical research charities, private companies and individuals. Guidance is given to those who are approached for funds to support medical research and reassurance given that duplicated research is not a waste of funds.

246. **National Council for Voluntary Organisations Information Department**
Joint Financing: Transfer of resources from health to social services (**NCVO Information Sheet; No. 24**)
NCVO, 1984, 4pp.

Joint finance is intended to facilitate the transfer of resources from hospital services to community care. Since April 1984, health authorities have been able to make payments to voluntary organisations and housing associations in addition to local authorities towards the housing and education of mentally and physically handicapped people.

This information sheet explains how joint finance works, how voluntary organisations can become involved in joint finance schemes and how it is working out in practice.

247. **National Federation of Housing Associations**
Special Projects and Joint Funding Arrangements
NFHA, 1983

A special project is one in which a housing association and voluntary organisation work together to provide accommodation for a group of people with special housing needs: single people, some disadvantaged families, elderly people, etc. This guide gives information about joint funding arrangements where the cost of a project is met jointly through the housing association administrative allowances system of the Department of the Environment, to pay for the housing element of the project, and another, either statutory or charitable, source to pay for the 'caring' element.

248. **Palliser, G.**
The Charitable Work of Hospital Contributory Schemes
British Hospitals Contributory Schemes Association (1948), 1984, 129pp.

Hospital contributory schemes provide insurance benefits supplementary to the provisions of the National Insurance and Health Service Acts. As a subsidiary function, the schemes provide funding for charities. In 1983, between them these schemes gave over £665,000 to charities.

This book gives accounts of the charitable work of hospital contributory schemes since 1948 including details of how much money has been given to which charities. The range of organisations to benefit is wide although all are linked to health in some way.

249. **Wales Council for Voluntary Action**
Care in the Community: A guide to funding for voluntary organisations in Wales
WCVA, 1983, 20pp.

In 1981 the Welsh Office issued a consultative document on the transfer of people from long term care into the community. In 1983 a circular was issued giving details of joint finance to promote this transfer, and promote joint planning and consultation between health and local authorities. The voluntary sector is eligible for this funding for both revenue and capital projects. The All Wales project to help mentally handicapped people and their families also includes the £ for £ scheme where voluntary funds are matched.

5.6 Sport

250. **Griffiths, H.**
Fund Raising for Sport: A guide for sports clubs
The Sports Council, 1985, 85pp.

This guide has been written specifically for sports clubs. It looks at a wide range of sources of grant aid and methods of raising money for sporting activities, including sponsored activities, jumble sales, lotteries and raising funds in the clubhouse. There are also sections on raising money to support promising individuals and for sport for disabled people. Appendices give information on grant aid and legislative differences in Northern Ireland, Wales and Scotland.

251. **Sceats, A.**
Sports and Leisure Club Management: A handbook for organisers
Macdonald and Evans, 1985, 207pp.

There are several relevant sections in this handbook. Chapter 2, 'Financial aspects of a club' goes into possible sources of income including subscriptions, bar sales, gaming machines, local authority assistance and hiring out facilities. Chapter 3, 'Funding large projects' looks at ways a club can raise funds by organising events and at sources of grant aid. An appendix gives a suggested layout for a fund-raising brochure.

252. **Sports Council**
Finance for Sports Facilities: How to get grants and loans for voluntary organisations.
Sports Council, 1985, Leaflet

This paper sets out the arrangements for the award of grants and interest-free loans by the Sports Council to local voluntary organisations for the provision of sports facilities. There is an outline of the facilities which can be aided, the amount of grant and loan and the conditions applying to them, and how to apply.

5.7 Women

253. **Berhane-Selassie, T.**
'Black women and the funding crisis'
Spare Rib, April 1985, No. 153, pp. 26–28

Some black women's groups get funding from local authorities. But the government's current policies are causing a crisis which many black women think will affect them differently from white women. The main reason for the difference is the criteria and conditions laid out by funding agencies even though theoretically these apply to all voluntary groups. Groups have to be 'non-political', but the very fact that black groups are organising is often seen as political. The process of funding has tried to force false structures on women's groups. Women's groups have started a dialogue on the problems of funding which has highlighted the need to look for alternative sources. A recent initiative is the setting up of a Charity Fund for black groups.

254. Bowman, M. and Norton, M.
Raising Money For Women: A survivors' guide
Bedford Square Press/NCVO, 1986, 128pp.

Women's groups face special problems when it comes to raising money. The abolition of the Greater London Council and metropolitan county councils has compounded their difficulties. The aim of this book is to give women's groups practical advice on raising funds. After giving a brief historical background to women's voluntary organisations and the current funding crisis they face, the authors go on to give advice on what needs to be done before a group starts to fund raise. They then go on to give information on the main sources of funds including local government, central government, quangos, trusts and companies. Ways of developing less conventional sources of funding are also covered. The book ends with how to develop strategies for change – how to increase women's influence and share of funding overall.

255. Equal Opportunities Commission
Grants for Equality: Research and education activities funded by the EOC, 1976–1981
EOC, 1981, 64pp.

Grants For Equality describes the research and projects the Equal Opportunities Commission has funded under the powers granted to it by the Sex Discrimination Act. Advice is given to applicants on the procedures to be followed and on the types of project considered eligible.

5.8 Youth and intermediate treatment

256. Youth Exchange Centre
Grants for Youth Exchanges
Youth Exchange Centre, Annual

The Youth Exchange Centre has funds to support youth exchanges between Britain and other countries in Europe, the Commonwealth, the Soviet Union and the USA. The types of exchange which may be eligible, the criteria for the award of a grant, the schemes in operation and lists of contacts are given.

257. Intermediate Treatment Fund
ITF Plan 1984–87
Intermediate Treatment Fund, 1984, 9pp.

The purpose of the Intermediate Treatment Fund is to encourage voluntary adult involvement in local programmes for young people in trouble with the law. It gives around £400,000 a year in grants to voluntary intermediate treatment projects. The *ITF Plan* describes the purpose of the Fund and sets out its objectives in relation to its main priority areas: its grant-making role; its role in supporting voluntary participation in intermediate treatment; its advocacy role; and generating resources in support of voluntary intermediate treatment services.

258. **National Association of Youth Clubs**
'Club funds'
Youth Clubs, Autumn 1982, No. 19, pp. 11–22

This special feature includes articles on local authority assistance to voluntary youth organisations; the experiences of three youth groups seeking money from other statutory sources; raising money from industry; raising money from trusts, with details of The Prince's Trust which is specifically for funding projects for 14–25 year olds; fund raising through organising events; and managing the club's money.

259. **Smith, D. R.**
GREA Today, Gone Tomorrow?: An analysis of the public funding of youth work 1981/82 to 1984/85
National Council for Voluntary Youth Services, 1984, 33pp.

This paper sets out in tabular form information on local education authorities Grant Related Expenditure Assessment (GREA) on the youth service. A table which compares support for voluntary youth organisations with total expenditure on the youth service reveals very different levels of support in different authorities. There appears to be no agreement as to what level of funding is necessary to meet the needs of young people and the youth service's knowledge and understanding of its own resources is poor. Recommendations for future improvement and action are made.

260. **Unell, J.**
Voluntary Action and Young People in Trouble: Funding
National Council for Voluntary Organisations, 1982, 17pp.

This booklet looks at funding for voluntary projects working with young people at risk or in trouble. It covers central government funding available from the DHSS, the Urban Programme, the Home Office and the DES. Local government powers to give financial support to voluntary organisations are described and funding from Quangos – the Intermediate Treatment Fund, the Commission for Racial Equality and Manpower Services Commission – is covered. Finally, advice on approaching charitable trusts is given along with details of 13 trusts known to fund such projects.

6 Financial Advantages of Charitable Status

261. **Ashdown, L. A. J.**
Rating Relief for Charitable Organisations
Shaw and Sons Ltd, 1982, 27pp.

This guide on rating relief for charitable organisations begins with the historical development of rating. It then goes on to talk about rating of churches and church halls, rating relief for charities, mandatory and discretionary relief and charities excluded from mandatory relief.

262. **Charities Aid Foundation**
'The Chancellor of charities'
Charity, April 1986, Vol. 3, No. 6, pp. 3–4, 20

This article looks at the 1986 budget proposals and speculates on the implications for charitable giving. The Charities Aid Foundation believes it to be the most reforming budget since the war. CAF forecasts it will result in millions of pounds of extra income for charities by opening up tax-effective charitable giving.

263. **Charities Aid Foundation**
Company Giving: The 1986 budget
CAF, 1986, Leaflet

This leaflet explains the new tax concessions introduced by the 1986 budget for company support of charities.

264. **Charities Aid Foundation**
Interest-Free Loans for the General Benefit of Charity
CAF, 1985, Leaflet

Making an interest-free loan is an effective way of giving to charity. This booklet explains how money lent to the Charities Aid Foundation by individuals or firms can benefit charities through the Seven-Day Loan Fund and Long-Term Loan Fund operated by CAF.

265. **Charities Aid Foundation**
Introducing Charities Aid Foundation
CAF, 1985, Leaflet

The Charities Aid Foundation was established to facilitate the distribution of money to charity and to promote the most effective ways of doing this. This leaflet briefly describes CAF's services to donors and charities. Separate publications describe particular services in more detail.

(See ref. Nos 71, 72, 73, 262, 263, 264, 266 and 267)

266. **Charities Aid Foundation**
Personal Charitable Trusts
CAF, 1984, 25pp.

The Charities Aid Foundation operates a service through which individuals can establish charitable trusts even where quite small amounts of money are involved. This booklet describes how the expense of setting up and running a trust can be largely avoided by using the services of the Charities Aid Foundation.

267. **Charities Aid Foundation**
Professional Management of Covenant Income
CAF, 1985, Leaflet

This leaflet explains the service the Charities Aid Foundation offers for taking over the administration of a charity's convenanted donations.

268. **Charities Aid Foundation**
Tax and Charities
Charities Aid Foundation in conjunction with Arthur Andersen & Co., 1983, 55pp.

Tax and Charities looks at the tax treatment of charities including tax advantages for donors to charity and deeds of convenant. Specimen tax recovery and convenant forms are given.

269. **Charity Commission**
Fiscal Benefits for Charities (TP19)
Charity Commission, 1984, 2pp.

This leaflet outlines the provision of fiscal benefits for charities under six headings: 1. income tax, corporation tax and capital gains tax; 2. capital transfer tax and development land tax; 3. value added tax; 4. stamp duty; 5. national insurance surcharge; 6. rates.

270. **Charity Commission**
The Official Custodian for Charities: Charity funds
Charity Commission, 1979, 4pp.

The Official Custodian for Charities was set up by Parliament to hold property in trust for charities and provide certain services to them free of charge. This leaflet describes the powers of the Official Custodian and the advantages for a charity in having its funds held by him (e.g. administration of recovery of tax is carried out free of charge; advice on investment is given).

271. Courtney, B.
Covenants: The art of tax-free giving
Northern Ireland Council for Voluntary Action, revised edition, 1985, 40pp.

The author's explanation of covenants is aimed at regular donors to charity and charity organisers. Covenants by individuals, companies, and trusts are covered and examples of the various covenant and tax claim forms included.

272. Craigmyle and Company Ltd and The Charities Aid Foundation
The Craigmyle Guide to Charitable Giving and Taxation
Craigmyle and Co Ltd in association with The Charities Aid Foundation, 10th edition, 1985, no pagination

This is a comprehensive guide to the financial benefits of charitable status. It has an updating service to inform purchasers of changes in legislation. It covers convenanted donations by individuals and companies, trading by charities, capital gains tax, capital transfer tax and value-added tax. Specimen convenant and tax recovery forms are given.

273. The Economist
'Britain's charities: towards a giving culture'
The Economist, 4 January 1986, Vol. 298, No. 7427, pp. 25–27

This article looks at tax concessions available to British charities and the arguments on both sides of the debate between charities and the government in which charities are asking for more concessions while the government feels it is already being generous. America, France, Germany, Italy and Canada all have tax systems more favourable to charities than the British system. At the time the article was written, charities were lobbying for reforms in the 1986 budget and some of their proposals are listed.

274. HM Customs and Excise
Value Added Tax: Charities (VAT Leaflet 701/1/84)
HM Customs and Excise, 1984, 11pp. (1986 edition in preparation)

This leaflet explains the VAT position of charities. The first part gives general information on how VAT affects charities. The second deals with the VAT position of some activities commonly carried out by charities, such as charity shops and meals-on-wheels. The third explains how VAT applies to donations, grants, membership subscriptions, etc. Annexes reproduce extracts from the relevant legislation which details reliefs from VAT and charitable activities which are zero-rated.

275. Home Office Voluntary Services Unit
Tax Benefits for Charities: Ways to stretch your charities' income
Home Office VSU, 1984, 7pp.

This booklet covers the range of tax reliefs available to charities, how tax relief increases a charity's income, tax incentives for donors, and points to further sources of information.

276. Kingdom, T. D.
Charities' Primary Guide (Revised) to Value-Added Tax
National Council for Voluntary Organisations, 1984, 28pp.

The complicated laws and regulations on VAT which affect charities are brought together in this guide. Its main purpose is to help charities decide whether or not they are required to register for VAT. Supplements are issued when there are changes in the regulations.

277. MacLachlan, R.
'Goodbye covenants – hello tax credits?'
Voluntary Action, September 1984, Vol. 2, No. 7, p. 11

Alternatives to the existing covenant system of donating to charity are explored, prompted by the belief that the Chancellor will lead a shift in financial policy which could radically change the pattern of fund raising. A further streamlining of the tax system looks imminent. An alternative to the present covenant system would be to end the present requirement that gifts be made over a long period of time. Another possibility would involve a tax credit system, as operated by British companies when calculating tax liability. Suitable tax incentives could lead to a dramatic increase in one-off donations.

278. National Council for Voluntary Organisations
Charities and Taxation (NCVO Information Sheet; No. 15)
NCVO, 1983, 5pp. (Revised edition due out in 1986)

The range of tax concessions to charities and donors to charities is summarised. Income tax and covenants, corporation tax and covenants, value added tax and other spending taxes, taxes on capital and rates are covered.

279. Norton, M.
Covenants: A practical guide to the tax advantages of giving
Directory of Social Change, 3rd edition, 1985, 132pp.

This guide explains how covenants work and what the advantages are of giving in this way both for individuals and for companies. It provides specimen documents which a charity can use or adapt when producing Deed of Covenant forms for its own use.

280. Norton, M.
A Guide to the Benefits of Charitable Status
Directory of Social Change, 1983, 170pp.
(Revised edition due to be published in December 1986)

This book brings together the benefits available to charities. The tax advantages of charitable status are explained, as are the conditions for eligibility for particular benefits. It covers rate reliefs and rebates; house to house and street collections; grants, donations and subscriptions; lotteries; company support for charity; charity trading; VAT reliefs; investment income.

281. Sinclair, W.
'Budget hand-outs for charities'
The Daily Telegraph, 19 April 1986, p. 23

The author explains the concessions to charities in the 1986 budget. He advises that deeds of covenant are still the most tax-efficient way of giving.

7 Law of Fund Raising

282. **Charity Commission**
The Provision of Alcohol on Charity Premises (TP 27)
Charity Commission, 1985, 8pp.

Providing alcohol on charity premises, either to improve facilities provided by the charity or as a ready source of funds, can be an attractive proposition. This leaflet looks at the problems it brings and what trustees may do within the limits of the law.

283. **Charity Commission**
Reports of the Charity Commissioners for England and Wales
HMSO, Annual

The Charity Commissioners' annual reports review events of importance to charities during the previous year. They include sections on changes in legislation and legal decisions affecting charities. Occasional guidance on specific topics is given, for example, the 1980 report looked at trading by or on behalf of charities and the 1984 report had appendices on fiscal benefits for charities and the law affecting charitable fund raising.

284. **Cracknell, D. G.**
Law Relating to Charities
Oyez Longman, 2nd edition, 1983, 270pp.

Chapter 10 on fund raising covers house to house collections, street collections, gaming, lotteries, pool betting, stage plays and film shows, 'Common good', Christmas card delivery, legacies and disabled persons. Chapter 11 focuses on the financial privileges of charities.

285. **Hayes, R. and Reason, J.**
Voluntary but not Amateur: A guide to the law for voluntary organisations and community groups
London Voluntary Service Council, 1985, 68pp.

The chapter on fund raising deals briefly with collections, lotteries and other forms of gaming, money from trusts, industry, local authorities, central government, quangos and Europe, and writing a proposal.

286. **Howell, D.**
Charities and Social Clubs: A handbook
National Federation of Community Organisations, 1984, 72pp.

Many voluntary organisations find bars an important source of funds. This handbook gives guidance on the legal, ethical and constitutional issues raised by the sale of alcohol by voluntary and community organisations.

287. **Kidd, H.**
Legislation Monitoring Service for Charities
LMSC, Quarterly

Subscribers to this service are sent quarterly reports which draw attention to recent changes in the law which affect charities and occasional notes on specific topics as they arise.

288. **National Council for Voluntary Organisations**
Alcohol in Village Halls
NCVO, 1983, 12pp.

This leaflet gives guidance to village hall committees who wish to make some arrangement for the provision of alcohol in their hall. In particular, it looks at the provision of a permanent bar and the requirements of charity law, licensing law and tax consequences in relation to this.

289. **National Council for Voluntary Organisations**
Lotteries and Gaming: Voluntary organisations and the law
Bedford Square Press/NCVO, 3rd edition reprinted with corrections, 1983, 42pp.

This guide explains the law relating to gaming, lotteries, competitions with prizes and similar activities. It will be of use to groups which organise, for example, bingo sessions, bridge and whist drives, tombolas or lotteries for fund-raising purposes.

290. **National Federation of Community Organisations**
Bars, Charities and the Law
NFCO, 1982, 38pp.

Bars, Charities and the Law gives guidance on how charity law, licensing and taxation relates to charities running a bar.

291. **Palmer, T.**
'Chancellor gets top prize in charity pool pay-out'
Charity, June 1985, Vol. 2, No. 8, pp. 6–7

The Cancer and Polio Research Fund runs its own football pool which gives the Fund a regular income derived from many people with a relatively small payout from each. A breakdown of income shows that the Exchequer receives in tax almost twice the amount the charity receives in donations. The rest of the money goes on administration costs and dividends.

292. Wade, F. *et al.*
CANS (Citizens Advice Notes): A service of information in two volumes compiled from authoritative sources
National Council for Voluntary Organisations, Cumulative; supplements are issued periodically to incorporate recent changes in law

CANS is a digest of current law in the UK. Sections relevant to charitable fund raising are included, for example, on street collections, house to house collections, lotteries and gaming.

293. Yeo, T.
Public Accountability and Regulation of Charities: The case for reform
The Spastics Society, 1983, 16pp.

Tim Yeo believes that the traditional image of charities is under threat and that public confidence needs to be maintained. His pamphlet sets out a programme of reform designed to improve the public accountability of charities and proposes a system of regulation as a measure to ease disquiet about how publicly donated money is spent. The programme for reform includes compulsory filing of annual accounts, widening of access to charity AGMs and a code of practice for fund raising and administration costs. The proposed system of self-regulation for charities would be by a Charity Council with moral rather than statutory powers and financially supported by the charities themselves.

8 Keeping Up With New Developments

294. **Charities Aid Foundation**
Charity Statistics
Charities Aid Foundation, Annual

Charity Statistics publishes statistical information on the financing of charities. Among the regular items are those giving figures on the top 200 corporate donors, the top 200 grant-making trusts and the top 200 grant-seeking charities. Each edition includes additional items on specific subjects. As an example, the 1984/85 edition reported on a major statistical survey of local authority financial support for charities.

(See also ref. nos 68, 90, 91, 197, 202 and 220)

295. **Fielding, N. (Editor)**
Voluntary Action
National Council for Voluntary Organisations, published weekly as a four page supplement in *New Society*
(Until the end of 1985, *Voluntary Action* was a separate publication issued 10 times a year.)

Voluntary Action has articles, news items, book reviews and information on forthcoming conferences and courses for the voluntary sector. It regularly includes items on fund raising and grant aid.

296. **Khuzwayo, W. (Editor)**
Voluntary Voice
London Voluntary Service Council, 8/9 issues a year

Since December 1985, *Voluntary Voice* has replaced two previously separate London Voluntary Service Council publications: *London Voluntary News* and *Community Work Service Newsletter*. It regularly has information on the funding of London's voluntary organisations. It was a particularly useful source of information for anyone needing to keep up with events during the abolition of the Greater London Council and continues to report on the effects of abolition on the funding of voluntary groups in London.

297. **Lawrie, S. (Executive Editor)**
Charity
Charities Aid Foundation, monthly

Charity aims to create a 'means of communication between the diverse interests of people who have to handle charitable funds as donors, as receivers and as administrators'. As the number of articles from *Charity* included in this bibliography will indicate, it is a useful source of information on the funding of the voluntary sector.

298. **Livingston Booth, D.** (Editor)
Philanthropy International
INTERPHIL, The International Standing Conference on Philanthropy,
Irregular, about three issues a year

Philanthropy International aims to reflect worldwide developments and activities
in the field of philanthropy. It carries articles, news items, conference reports and
book reviews.

299. **Turnbull, M.** (Editor)
Third Sector
Scottish Council for Community and Voluntary Organisations, Bi-monthly

This magazine about the voluntary sector in Scotland regularly carries news
items on the funding of Scottish voluntary organisations.

300. **Voluntary Movement Group**
VMG News
Voluntary Movement Group, Bi-monthly

The Voluntary Movement Group was set up in 1968 with the object of bringing
together those engaged in public relations and fund-raising on behalf of charities
and voluntary organisations to improve and extend their knowledge and
exchange information and experience. *VMG News* is a source of information on
events and news of interest to fund raisers, including forthcoming seminars,
courses and recent publications.

301. **Williams, L.** (Editor)
Network Wales
Wales Council for Voluntary Action, monthly

This magazine for Welsh voluntary organisations regularly carries items on
funding.

302. **Windsor, M. and Evers, C.** (Editors)
Voluntary Forum Abstracts
National Council for Voluntary Organisations and The Volunteer Centre,
Bi-monthly

This is an abstracting service giving information on recently published books,
pamphlets, reports, government publications and journal articles on the voluntary sector. It provides:
a) an effective way of keeping up to date with new literature on a regular basis
b) easy access to finding out what has been written on a particular topic of
   relevance to voluntary organisations within the last few years.
   It is also available online on the London Residuary Body Research Library's
(formerly the Greater London Council Research Library) database, Acompline.

Useful Addresses

Books issued by large commercial publishers are usually widely available and can be bought through booksellers or via the publisher's distributor. With the exception of these publishers, this list contains the addresses of the organisations which published the documents listed in this guide.

The addresses marked with an asterisk * are of organisations which offer services, such as information, advice and training, to voluntary organisations.

* **Action Resource Centre,** 3rd Floor, Cap House, 9–12 Long Lane, London EC1A 9HD, Tel. 01-726 8987
ARC aims to encourage and help industry and commerce in working with voluntary organisations to meet the needs of local communities. It offers a free service to companies wishing to second staff to community projects.

***Association for Business Sponsorship of the Arts,** 2 Chester Street, London SW1X 7BB, Tel. 01-235 9781
ABSA gives help and advice on the benefits of sponsorship to businesses and the arts.

Association of Medical Research Charities, c/o Development Trust for the Young Disabled, Royal Hospital and Home for Incurables, West Hill, London SW15 3SW

Attorney General, Royal Courts of Justice, Strand, London WC2A 2LL

Belfast Simon Community, PO Box 90, Belfast BT1 1ST

Berkshire Charities Combined Fundraising Association, c/o Community Council for Berkshire, Venture Fair, Lower Padworth, Reading RG7 4JR

Brighton Council for Voluntary Service, 17 Ditchling Rise, Brighton, East Sussex BN1 4QL

British Council of Churches, Race, Pluralism and Community Group, 2 Eaton Gate, London SW1W 9BL

British Hospitals Contributory Schemes Association (1948), 4th Floor, Refuge Buildings, Baldwin Street, Bristol BS1 1SE

British Institute of Management, Management House, Cottingham Road, Corby, Northants NN17 1TT

*Business in the Community, 227a City Road, London EC1V 1JU, Tel. 01-253 3716
BIC promotes community involvement by industry, commerce and the professions.

Calouste Gulbenkian Foundation, 98 Portland Place, London W1N 4ET

Centre for Policy Studies, 8 Wilfred Street, London SW1E 6PL

Centre on Environment for the Handicapped, 126 Albert Street, London NW1 7NF

*Charities Advisory Trust, Radius Works, Back Lane, Hampstead, London NW3 1HL, Tel. 01-794 9835
(Previously known as the Charity Trading Advisory Group)
The Trust offers help and advice on charity trading.

*Charities Aid Foundation, 48 Pembury Road, Tonbridge, Kent TN9 2JD, Tel. 0732 356323
CAF was set up to help and co-ordinate the raising and distribution of funds to other charities. It aims to make people's giving as effective as possible and does this through a range of financial and information services to donors and charities.

*Charity Commission, St. Albans House, 57–60 Haymarket, London SW1Y 4QX, Tel. 01-210 3000
The general functions of the Charity Commission include promoting the effective use of charitable resources by giving advice to trustees.

*Charity Information Bureaux
Charity Information Bureaux collect information on grant-making trusts, and sometimes on other sources of funding, in order to advise organisations within their area on where it is most appropriate for them to apply to for support. Those currently in existence are:
Birmingham Charities Information Bureau, 168 Corporation Street, Birmingham B4 6TF, Tel. 021-236 8250
Charities Information Service (Sussex), c/o Chapel Royal, North Street, Brighton BN1 1EA, Tel. 0273 21398
Humberside Charities Information Bureau, Community Council of Humberside, 14 Market Place, Howden, Goole, Humberside DN14 7BJ, Tel. 0430 30904
South Yorkshire Charity Information Service Trust, 40 Trippett Lane, Sheffield S1 4EL, Tel. 0742 731765
Tyne & Wear and Northumberland Charities Information Service, Mea House, Ellison Place, Newcastle upon Tyne NE1 8XS, Tel. 0632 327445
West Yorkshire Charities Information Bureau, 11 Upper York Street, Wakefield WF1 3LQ, Tel. 0924 382120

Wiltshire Charities Information Bureau, Andil House, Court Street, Trowbridge, Wilts BA14 8BR, Tel. 022-146 8848

The Chartered Institute of Public Finance and Accountancy, 3 Robert Street, London WC2N 6BH

Christian Aid, PO Box No. 1, London SW9 8BH

Commission for Racial Equality, Elliott House, 10–12 Allington Street, London SW1E 5EH

Commission of the European Communities, London Office, 8 Storey's Gate, London SW1P 3AT

Community Council of Suffolk, Alexandra House, Rope Walk, Ipswich IP4 2JS

Conservative Political Centre, 32 Smith Square, London SW1P 3HH

Consortium on Opportunities for Volunteering, 26 Bedford Square, London WC1B 3HU

*Council for Charitable Support, c/o Charities Aid Foundation, 48 Pembury Road, Tonbridge, Kent TN9 2JD, Tel. 0732 356323
The Council was set up in 1985 by a group of business people with the objective of encouraging wider understanding of the need for financial and other support for voluntary organisations. It gives priority to furthering the means of attracting such support. It is in the process of compiling *Company Support for Charities: Guidelines for good management.*

Councils for Voluntary Service National Association, 26 Bedford Square, London WC1B 3HU

Countryside Commission, John Dower House, Crescent Place, Cheltenham, Glos GL50 3RA

Craigmyle & Co. Ltd, The Grove, Harpenden, Herts AL5 1AH

Croydon Guild of Voluntary Organisations, Eldon House, 78 Thornton Road, Thornton Heath, Croydon CR4 6BA

Department of Employment, Caxton House, Tothill Street, London SW1H 9NF

Department of the Environment, 2 Marsham Street, London SW1P 3EB

Department of Health and Social Security, Alexander Fleming House, Elephant & Castle, London SE1 6BY

Development Commission, 11 Cowley Street, Westminster, London SW1P 3NA

*Directory of Social Change, Radius Works, Back Lane, Hampstead, London NW3 1HL, Tel. 01-435 8171

The Directory of Social Change provides information, publishing, research and training services to the voluntary sector. It issues a wide range of publications on fund raising as well as organising courses on raising money.

Equal Opportunities Commission, Overseas House, Quay Street, Manchester M3 3HN

*Ethical Investment, Research and Information Service, 9 Poland Street, London W1V 3DG, Tel. 01-439 4771
EIRIS provides a service to investors who wish to avoid certain forms of investment they regard as undesirable.

Hackney Community Action, 380 Old Street, London EC1

HAY-MSL Management Consultants Group Ltd, 52 Grosvenor Gardens, London SW1W 0AU

HM Customs and Excise, King's Beam House, 39–41 Mark Lane, London EC3R 7HE

HM Treasury, Parliament Street, London SW1P 3AG

IBIS Information Services Ltd, Waterside, Lowbell Lane, London Colney, Herts AL2 1DX

Independent Broadcasting Authority, 70 Brompton Road, London SW3 1EY

*Institute of Charity Fundraising Managers, 14 Bloomsbury Square, London WC1, Tel. 01-831 7399
The Institute aims to improve and maintain high standards in the fundraising profession. It has produced a code of practice for charity fundraising managers.

The Institute of Economic Affairs, 2 Lord North Street, London SW1P 3LD

Intermediate Treatment Fund, 33 King Street, London WC2E 8JD

Islington Bus Co., Community Resource Centre, Palmer Place, London N7 8DH

*Legislation Monitoring Service for Charities, Harry Kidd, 7 Market Street, Woodstock, Oxford.
LMSC monitors current legislation and proposals for legislation that may affect charities. (See ref. no. 287)

The Liberal Party, 1 Whitehall Place, London SW1A 2HE

Liverpool Council for Voluntary Service, 14 Castle Street, Liverpool L2 0NJ

Local Development Agencies Development Fund, 26 Bedford Square, London WC1B 3HU

London Voluntary Service Council, 68 Chalton Street, London NW1 1JR

Manchester Council for Voluntary Service, The Gaddum Centre, 274 Deansgate, Manchester M3 4FT

Manpower Services Commission, Moorfoot, Sheffield S1 4PQ

*National Council for Voluntary Organisations, 26 Bedford Square, London WC1B 3HU, Tel. 01-636 4066

The departments within NCVO which may be able to offer advice and information on different aspects of funding include:

Appeals Department – can give information on fund raising, on fiscal considerations, on sources of guidance on fund raising and on fund raising consultants.

Community Schemes Unit – supports organisations involved with the Youth Training Scheme.

Employment Unit – promotes and supports the involvement of voluntary organisations in employment issues, including involvement with the Community Programme and Voluntary Projects Programme.

International Affairs – can provide information about European Community funds available to voluntary organisations, and in particular on the European Social Fund.

Library – has a collection of material on the voluntary sector including publications on funding.

Organisation Development Unit (Ethnic Minorities) – was set up to meet the organisational and developmental needs of black organisations. Among other things, it offers advice and information on funding.

United Funds – encourages the setting up of payroll-giving schemes.

Urban Unit – supports the work of inner city organisations including giving guidance on the Urban Programme.

National Council for Voluntary Youth Services, Wellington House, 29 Albion Street, Leicester LE1 6GD

National Federation of Community Organisations, 8–9 Upper Street, London N1 0PQ

National Federation of Housing Associations, 175 Gray's Inn Road, London WC1X 8UP

National Federation of Self-Help Organisations, 150 Townmead Road, London SW6 2RA

National Youth Bureau, 17–23 Albion Street, Leicester LE1 6GD

Nature Conservancy Council, Northminster House, Peterborough PE1 1UA

*Northern Ireland Council for Voluntary Action, 2 Annadale Avenue, Belfast BT7 3JR, Tel. 0232 640011
NICVA aims to promote, support and facilitate voluntary action in Northern Ireland through, for example, the provision of information and training services.

Northern Ireland Trusts Group, c/o Olderfleet Room, Howard House, 1 Brunswick Street, Belfast BT2 7GE

Northern Ireland Voluntary Trust, Olderfleet Room, Howard House, 1 Brunswick Street, Belfast BT2 7GE

Opportunities for Volunteering in Wales, Llys Ifor, Crescent Road, Caerffili CF8 1XL

Phillips and Drew, 120 Moorgate, London EC2M 6XP

Policy Studies Insitute, 100 Park Village East, London NW1 3SR

Scottish Community Education Council, Atholl House, 2 Canning Street, Edinburgh EH3 8EG

*Scottish Council for Community and Voluntary Organisations, 18–19 Claremont Crescent, Edinburgh EH7 4QD, Tel. 031-556 3882
SCCVO provides information, training and support for the voluntary sector in Scotland.

Shaw and Sons Ltd, Shaway House, London SE26

Shell Better Britain Campaign, Nature Conservancy Council, Northminster House, Peterborough PE1 1UA

The Spastics Society, 12 Park Crescent, London W1N 4EQ

Sports Council, 16 Upper Woburn Place, London WC1H 0QP

United Biscuits, Syon Lane, Isleworth, Middx TW7 5NN

United Way of Merseyside, 8 Nelson Road, Edge Hill, Liverpool L69 7AA

University of Bristol, School for Advanced Urban Studies, Rodney Lodge, Grange Road, Bristol BS8 4EA

Voluntary Action Lewisham, 120 Rushey Green, Catford, London SE6 4HQ

Voluntary Action Westminster, 1 St. Mary's Terrace, London W2 1SU

*Voluntary Movement Group, 54 Church Street, Tisbury, Salisbury, Wilts SP3 6NH, Tel. 0747 870490
The VMG aims to bring together those engaged in public relations and fund raising on behalf of charities and voluntary organisations, improve and extend their knowledge and exchange information and experience. It holds meetings and seminars and publishes a newsletter. *(See ref. No. 300)*

*Voluntary Services Unit, Home Office, Queen Anne's Gate, London SW1H 9AT, Tel. 01-213 4376
The VSU acts as a link between voluntary organisations and government departments. It can advise voluntary organisations on the best points of contact within other departments.

The Volunteer Centre, 29 Lower King's Road, Berkhamsted, Herts HP4 2AB

*Wales Council for Voluntary Action, Llys Ifor, Crescent Road, Caerffili, CF8 1XL, Tel. 0222 869224
WCVA aims to promote, support and facilitate voluntary action and community development in Wales. At the beginning of 1986, WCVA set up a Charities Information Unit to help organisations secure funding for their work.

Will to Charity Ltd, 10 Beauchamp Place, London SW3

Young Friends Central Committee, Friends House, Euston Road, London NW1 2BJ

Youth Exchange Centre, c/o Central Bureau for Educational Visits and Exchanges, Seymour Mews House, Seymour Mews, London W1H 9PE

Author Index

Numbers refer to entry numbers and not page numbers.

Title Index

101

Subject Index

This index should help if you are trying to find out about a particular subject. It will lead you to publications which contain information on that subject. If, for example, you mant to know more about using fund-raising consultants, then references, 5, 8, 10 and 117 to 120 will be of interest.

Passing references and short passages on a topic are not indexed.

Royal Institute of British Architects
232

Schools, fund raising through 5, 69,
70, 75
Scotland, funding for voluntary
organisations 27, 136, 178,
179, 191, 192, 299
Secondment of staff 88, 89, 96, 97,
102, 103, 108, 110, 111
Section 137, Local Government Act
1972 191–4, 204, 205
Short-term funding 142, 144, 154,
167, 168, 182, 183, 186–8
Sponsored events 5, 9, 10, 12, 51,
75, 250
Sponsorship (commercial) 9, 86, 98,
108, 109, 219, 220, 230
Sport, funding for 32, 98, 250–2
Sports Council 147, 151, 250–2
Statutory funding see Grant aid
Street collections 5, 10, 13, 18, 74,
80, 280, 284, 292
Northern Ireland 9
Suppliers of fund-raising stationery
and equipment 29, 51, 52

Taxation of charities 7, 25, 261–86
Tax reliefs
capital gains tax 272, 284
capital transfer tax 10, 77, 78,
268, 272, 284
company giving 101, 219, 263,
268, 272, 278
covenants 10, 23, 110, 219, 268,
271, 272, 277–81
income tax 10, 71, 73, 268,
271–3, 278, 279, 284
legacies 5, 10, 72, 77, 78
rates 21, 23, 261, 268, 278, 280,
284
value added tax 10, 21, 22, 219,
268, 272, 274, 276, 278, 280, 284
Television and radio 5, 9, 34,
39–42, 44, 45, 48, 49, 225, 228
Third World see Overseas Aid
Trading 5, 8–10, 23, 55–8, 272, 280

Christmas cards 5, 55
Training projects see Employment
and training projects
Trusts 5, 11, 12, 16, 18, 20, 21, 24,
121–41, 239, 254, 258, 260, 294
charity information bureaux 121,
123, 124, 132, 141
community trusts 112–16
Northern Ireland 9, 122, 134
policy on grant-giving 124, 125,
127, 129, 139, 140, 165
Scotland 27, 136, 299
Wales 116, 301

United Way see Payroll giving
Urban Programme 147, 151, 158,
161, 163, 177, 178, 185, 239,
241, 254

Value added tax 10, 21, 22, 219,
268, 272, 274, 276, 278, 280, 284
Voluntary Projects Programme 147,
173–5, 180–3
Voluntary Services Unit 3, 5, 147,
156, 167, 170
Volunteer projects
funding for 148, 157, 160, 162,
166, 173–5
Northern Ireland 153
Wales 155

Wales funding for voluntary
organisations 31, 116, 155,
184, 185, 249, 301
Waste collections 10, 30
Welsh Office 184, 249
Wills see legacies
Women's organisations, funding
for 210, 253–5
Writing a funding application 11,
12, 22, 24, 122, 124, 130, 132,
133, 135, 137, 138, 147, 164,
215–18, 251, 254

Youth Training Scheme 147, 174,
176
Youth projects, funding for 256–60

108